BRITISH AND NATIVE COCHIN

BRITISH
AND
NATIVE COCHIN

LAWSON, CHARLES A.

GYAN

Published by

Gyan Publishing House
5, Ansari Road
Daryaganj, New Delhi-110002
Phone: 011-47034999, 9811692060
E-mail: books@gyanbooks.com

Distribution Network
gyanbooks.com
India, USA, Canada, UK, Australia, France

ISBN : 978-81-212-3157-2 (PB)
First Published, 1861

2nd Impression 2020

Printed at: Gyan Press, Delhi.

British and Native Cochin
Author: Lawson, Charles A.

BRITISH AND NATIVE COCHIN.

BY

CHARLES ALLEN LAWSON.

(Second Edition.)

LONDON:

NISSEN & PARKER, 43, MARK LANE.

1861.

Inscribed to

ALFRED.

CONTENTS.

CHAPTER I.

HISTORICAL SKETCH.

CHAPTER II.

DESCRIPTIVE SKETCH.

CHAPTER III.

THE BAZAAR.

CHAPTER IV.

THE MALABARS.

CHAPTER V.

THE MALABARS.

CHAPTER VI.

THE RAJAH.

CONTENTS.

Cochin, May 17th, 1860.

BRITISH COCHIN.

CHAPTER I.

HISTORICAL SKETCH.

Discovery of America—Influence of Queen Isabella—Vasco de Gama's first expedition to India—Lands at Calicut—Reception by Zamorin—Cabral discovers Brazil—Touches at Cochin—De Gama's second expedition—Erects factory at Cochin—Albuquerque fortifies it—His conquests—De Gama appointed Viceroy—Dies in Cochin—His character—Court removed to Goa—Bigotry of the Portuguese—Expulsion by Dutch—Cochin captured—Trade, prosperity, habits, and fall of Dutch—Cochin surrendered to the English—Importance of its harbour.

It is now more than three centuries and a half since Columbus, by the discovery of a Continent beyond the Atlantic, re-excited the spirit of adventure throughout Europe. Actuated chiefly by a desire to reach the western coast of that El Dorado, which, from the time of the Crusaders, had supplied the North with the most esteemed luxuries of the East, he was also influenced by an ambition to diminish the power of Venice to the advantage of Spain. A native of Genoa, he had doubtless heard again and again of her former greatness in the possession of a share of the Indian trade; and had, consequently, deeply imbibed that jealousy of her rival's superiority which existed more or less in every country during the fifteenth century. His specious representations of the probability of land beyond the Ocean at first met with cold bigoted contempt; but being at length fortunate enough to inoculate a benevolent friar with his schemes, he was, through this saintly introduction afforded the opportunity of explaining his great views to Queen Isabella, who, with further discernment than any of her nobles, gave him the whole weight of her influence, and the assistance of her private means to promote his object.

Immediately Europe was informed of the existence of new fields of wealth, little inducement was required to stimulate research; and England, in discovering North America; Portugal in turning the Cape of Good Hope, and extending her power to India, China, &c.; and Holland, in developing the wealth of the Southern Seas; are entitled to feelings of pride in the energy of their subjects. But it is to Spain's great Queen ISABELLA that the credit must be given of originating these vast expeditions—ruinous however as have been the effects to her country of that wealth she was so mainly instrumental in introducing into Europe.

The King of Portugal was not slow to catch the spirit of his great neighbour; but, being unable to adopt the same route in search for India as Columbus pursued, he wisely determined to plan a new one — due South. BARTHOLOMEW DIAZ had recently returned with the information that Africa was terminated by a Cape; and although his sailors would not permit him to extend his investigations far up the Eastern Coast, he had been enabled justly to conclude that this was the most direct road to India. VASCO DE GAMA was appointed to the command of the expedition, and with three small vessels, sixty men, and the anxious hopes of his country, he set sail from Lisbon on the 8th July 1497—four years after Europe had been startled by Columbus' great discoveries.

De Gama appears to have suffered distress of weather in rounding the Cape, and would seem to have crept up the Eastern Coast of Africa very timorously until he arrived off Melinda in Zanquebar, and obtained the services of a Guzerat pilot well acquainted with the Indian Ocean. The little squadron safely crossed to the new Continent, arriving off Calicut on the 20th May 1498. Prescott is very happy in his imagination of the feelings of Cortes and Pizarro when they first beheld the abundantly fertile kingdoms of Mexico and Peru; but, strangely gratifying as those feelings must have been, it is conceivable that Vasco de Gama experienced yet more delight in the discovery of India, the land of spices, jewels, grains, sugars, cotton, silk, indigo, tobacco, woods, ivory, drugs, and perfumes.

Calicut was then the most important town on the Western coast of India. Its immense export trade with Persia, Arabia, Egypt, and (by the agency of Venice) with Europe, was in the hands of the Moors and Arabs, generally a most lawless herd, jealous to a degree of their interests, and cruelly disposed towards any rivals. Vasco de Gama immediately signified his intention to land and attempt to propitiate the Zamorin, or King of Calicut; and, disregarding alike the entreaties of his brother and crew, he bravely made his way ashore, leaving instructions that in case of his fall, the expedition should at once return with the news of his discoveries. The Zamorin received him at first courteously; but as De Gama had provided himself with presents of a most trifling value, his tone soon altered into one of intimidation, and it required all De Gama's plausibility to paint the alliance of the King of Portugal as the greatest blessing, and his anger as the greatest misfortune which could befall Calicut. A few civilities were interchanged, and De Gama, apparently satisfied with his reception, returned to Lisbon after an absence of two years and two months. The King of Portugal, highly delighted with De Gama's success, proclaimed him Admiral of the Indian, Persian, and Arabian seas.

Pedro Alvaraz de Cabral was now dispatched to make further investigations in the new lands. Confident by the success of his predecessors in crossing oceans, he boldly stood out to sea, and was rewarded by the discovery, on the 3rd May, 1500, of Brazil, of which he took possession in the name of his sovereign, and sent home several surveys and reports of the country. Americus Vesputius was sent out at once to secure this new seizure, and discharged his duties so creditably that the King, as an inducement to others, permitted the Continent to be called America, after his Christian name. Cabral, who thus lost that chance of being immortalized which in justice belonged to Columbus, provided himself with the seeds of some valuable Brazilian fruits, and at length arrived off Cochin on 24th December 1500. After some preliminary negociations with the Rajah, Cabral proceeded to Calicut, established a small factory, placed a few Portuguese in charge, and returned home. Hardly had his ships disappeared on the horizon than the natives rose, massacred every white man, and destroyed the station. For this act of cruelty the inhabitants of the coast suffered years of misery; and though we can well imagine that had they not afforded a pretext, the Portuguese would have made one as villainous as the majority of pioneers of civilization have been guilty of, it is to be lamented that the initiative of cruelty was taken by the, as yet, uninjured native. In stirring the whole Portuguese nation to take vengeance on the criminals, the country was soon brought under the dominion of the Whites; and the Portuguese may date their ascendancy in India as surely from the smoking ruins of the factory in Calicut, as the British theirs from the Black Hole at Calcutta.

Immediately after the news arrived of the massacre, another expedition was resolved upon, and placed under the command of De Gama. He was provided with a well-equipped fleet of twenty sail, which he arranged in three squadrons; the largest of which, consisting of ten vessels, he himself directed. With this detachment he arrived off Calicut in 1502; seized, plundered, and scuttled a richly-laden ship belonging to the Sultan of Egypt, after having murdered the crew; blockaded the town, cut out the majority of the vessels in the harbour, and inflicted such loss upon the foreign merchants, that the Zamorin was forced to treat. Still De Gama would not consider any terms until the murderers of his countrymen were placed in his hands, and this being refused after a truce of three days, he cannonaded the town and barbarously hung fifty Malabar sailors found in the captured vessels. The Zamorin saw half his capital in ruins, and yet would not surrender; so, after exhausting his power of doing mischief, De Gama set sail for Cochin, a neighbouring province, between the Rajah of which and the Sovereign of Calicut a war had long existed. By offering his assistance and protection, and declaring the power of Portugal to be irresistible, he easily brought about an offensive and defensive alliance with the Rajah, receiving on this consideration permission to establish a factory at the entrance of the Backwater. He shortly returned to Lisbon, was brilliantly received, and created Count of Videqueyra.

ALPHONSO D' ALBUQUERQUE, who had some time previously departed to assume the command, arrived at Cochin on the 2nd September, 1503, happily in time to check the progress of the Zamorin, and reassure the Rajah's throne. For this valuable assistance, and by representing that it would be an insuperable bar to the Zamorin's sea operations, he was permitted to fortify the little settlement. Commanding the highway to the capital, and strengthening themselves against attack on the land side, the Portuguese held most important arguments for the Rajah's good-will, and early showed their intention to exercise them. Such misplaced confidence and want of reflection on the part of the Rajah is inexplicable; forming a miserable contrast to the indomitable resolution of the Aztecs and Incas, and to the unconquerable ambition of Holkar, Hyder, and Tippo.

Invested with the command in chief of both army and navy, Albuquerque appeared again on the coast in 1506, with a fleet of sixteen vessels. From that period until 1515 he pursued an unbroken series of conquest in Cannanore, Goa, the Persian Gulf, the Malaccas, &c.,

and established that wide dominion in the East which the Portuguese enjoyed for about a century and a half. He was then superseded by two of his lieutenants, and in the bitterness of his spirit cried, "What! Soarez governor! Vascancelles and Pereira, whom I sent home as criminals, sent out again in posts of honor! I have gained the hate of men for the love of the King, and am disgraced by the King for the love of men. To the grave! miserable old man, to the grave! It is time." He died shortly afterwards.

Alphonso d'Albuquerque, governor of the Indies, was a bold-minded man, ambitious for his country's glory, unscrupulous as to its attainment. Unsullied by those peculant traits which disgraced Cortes and Pizarro, he possessed Clive's avarice for the enrichment of his followers; as considerate a commander as Marlborough to the obedient, he had Napoleon's vindictive feelings towards the rebellious; with the heroic courage of Alvarado, or Murat, he lacked the discretion of Cæsar, and those great principles that peculiarly distinguished Wellington. After raising his couutry to a foremost position in the world, he was destroyed by that royal jealousy which has frequently been the reward of the great in all ages. Truly England, remembering her prosecution of Warren Hastings, cannot cast a stone at her neighbours, yet she can congratulate herself that her annals are not so shamefully seared with ingratitude towards enterprising valour in her behalf, as are those of Spain and Portugal.

In 1524 the importance of the Indian possessions had so increased, that King John III. of Portugal determined to establish a viceroyalty in the East. Vasco de Gama, who had been living in titled ease for twenty years, was prevailed upon to proceed again to the field of his fame; and arrived at Cochin towards the close of 1525, as the first European Viceroy of India. He came, however, but to lay his bones on oriental shores, for he died in December of the same year, after a far longer tenure of Fortune's smiles than the majority of discoverers enjoy. His remains were interred in the chancel of the Franciscan Church at Cochin, but were removed thirteen years afterwards to Portugal, and were deposited with great pomp in the Royal Chapel at Lisbon.

Vasco de Gama, Count of Videqueyra and first Viceroy of Portuguese India, was one of those men whom Fortune delights in cherishing. Profiting by the discovery of Diaz, he sailed over his bones at the Cape of Good Hope, and reaped the credit of having originated the route; proceeding up the Coast of Africa, he experienced little difficulty, peril, or hardship in crossing the Indian Ocean, and in finding that land on which the greedy desires of all Europe were set. His successors proved the value of his discoveries, and thus increased his importance with his countrymen. He died on the field of his glory, invested with the highest honors his King could confer. From the highly coloured portrait in Greenwich Hospital, we imagine him to have been a man above the middle stature, with a finely developed head, and pleasing expression of countenance; but at this period Titian had not instructed the world in the art of painting with fidelity.

De Gama had brought with him a sealed letter from the King, appointing a successor to the Viceroyalty after his demise. Thus no delay was caused, and Henrique

Menezez was at once invested. Goa was now being built, and as soon as it was sufficiently convenient the Viceroy removed his Court from Cochin.

FRANCIS XAVIER, — the dearest friend of Ignatius Loyola, the founder of the Order of Jesuits,—arrived at Goa in 1542, and for ten years was indefatigable in his exertions to proselytize the heathen of the Malabar Coast, Cochin, &c. He was a true Missionary, though his doctrines were erroneous; neither before nor since his appearance in India has the Roman Catholic Church had one champion to excel him in honesty of purpose, in persevering energy, in Christian benevolence. He died on the Island of Sancian, within sight of China, under a tropical sun, cruelly deserted by all his companions. Eight years after his death the Inquisition was established at Goa, with the vilest of those characteristics which even now make one's blood run cold in thinking about. The native Syrian Christians, an inoffensive and devout sect, were cruelly persecuted; the heathen suffered injustice of the direst form; and the merciless bigotry of the settlers to impose religion on them by force became so intolerable, that, even had the Dutch not appeared, the Portuguese must have been expelled from the country by an alliance of the Jews, Turks, and Infidels. During the century and a half following their settlement in Cochin, they erected the handsome Church of Santa Cruz, and shortly obtained from Pius IV. permission to style it a Cathedral, on the appointment of Themuds to the Bishopric of these parts. Several monasteries and small churches were built from time to time, and great attention was given to the fortifications. It does not appear that they promoted any considerable trading connexion with natives; and being indifferent to the grafting of their power on the interests of the inhabitants, its fall was sudden and irrecoverable. Their bigoted attention to the spiritual, and their avaricious envy of the temporal welfare of the people, resulted in the Portuguese losing possession of the richest countries in the world. It was natural, it was just it should be so, however unworthy the agents of retribution might have been.

The Portuguese having thus by cruelty and avarice alienated the sympathies of their native subjects, were dispossessed of their conquests as soon as another European power appeared to dispute the tenure. Holland, long subjected to Spain, had at length recovered her freedom, and early fitted out expeditions against her rivals' settlements in the East. Though devoid of the romantic ardour in such enterprises which distinguished the Spaniard and Portuguese, the Dutchman possessed that persevering resolution in the pursuit of an object, which, regarding failures as incentives to redoubled exertions, must command success in the long run. Destitute of bigotry, he regarded every new conquest in proportion as it affected his commercial interests; and in the furtherance of trade he was perfectly indifferent to the welfare of the natives. Like the Anglo-Indian of old, he generally left his religion at the Cape, to be reassumed on his return home; and consequently we find his inner life in India to have often been most unworthy of an European.

The Dutch first obtained a footing in Ceylon, and strengthened it; conciliated the native princes, and progressed slowly, but surely, over that beautiful Island, until in 1656 Colombo was forced to capitulate, and their conquest completed. Its commercial advantages were rapidly developed, but the presence of their rivals on the mainland exposed them to such continual danger that measures were at once taken to obtain universal supremacy. After Negapatam on the Coromandal, and Quilon and Cranganore on the Malabar coast, had been captured, the Dutch forces under Van Goens advanced against Cochin A.D. 1662. The assault was bravely made, but as bravely resisted; and after a fearful slaughter of Nairs in the Ranee's palace, the Dutch were forced back to their boats; and the Monsoon setting in shortly after, they withdrew to Quilon. The Portuguese were delighted beyond measure with their victory, eagerly anticipated the recovery of their possessions in Ceylon and on the Coast, and neglected to strengthen themselves against the enemy's return. But in October the Dutch appeared again before the town, with better respect for the difficulty of the undertaking, and firmer determination to proceed methodically to work. Assisted by a petty Rajah of the district and by the Jews in the town, the assault was repeated on the 6th January, 1663, and attended with every success. The Portuguese garrison was transported to Goa; such of the inhabitants as had the opportunity returned home, whilst the remainder and poorer submitted to their conquerors, and were gradually degenerated by contact with native blood, their descendants being now only recognisable by their grandiloquent patronymics, and their firm adhesion to their ancestors' superstition and creed. As was only likely, a strong feeling of pitiable contempt was bred in the Dutch for their predecessors in the country, and even in the present day the latter are hardly in caste. With Cochin the Portuguese power fell in India, after a supremacy of one hundred and sixty years, for precisely the same causes as brought about its overthrow in America. Ignorant of the power of deriving solid advantages from their conquests by honest industry, they satisfied their avarice at the expense of the natives, and, so soon as one field was drained, proceeded to exhaust the next, until by making all subjects foes they paved the way for the successful advance of the first European antagonist.

The Dutch were not long in discovering the numerous facilities offered by Cochin as a place of trade with the Coast, Surat, Arabia, China, and Europe. In return for pepper, cardamoms, woods, cocoanuts, coir yarns, &c., they imported gums, opium, cotton, piece goods, spices, and tea. The place prospered in their possession; the fortifications were repaired, the streets replanned, the moat cleared out, the walls planted with tulip trees, which also served to make an "unter den Linden" through the town, and no expense spared to beautify it consonant with the conservative taste of Dutchmen. The Cathedral was turned into a storehouse, the churches swept of every papistical emblem, and with a recollection of the many ills they had suffered at the hands of the priests, rigorous proceedings were at first enforced against the Roman Catholic faith, though as soon as the conquest was assured there was greater toleration. The Establishment consisted of the Governor, his council of eight Burghers, the Head Merchant, the Commandant, the Fiscal, Storekeeper, Bookkeeper, Cashier, Secretary, &c.

Entirely devoted to commercial pursuits, the Dutch

relieved the natives from the bigoted tyranny of their predecessors, but soon, by their grasping avarice, destroyed the popular opinion in their favour, and thus afforded the English those advantages which had contributed so materially to their own success. Their habits were grossly animal; rising at about six, the Dutchman took a stroll or lounged in his verandah with a huge pipe in his mouth until seven, when coffee, meat, &c. were brought him by a slave, his pipe replenished, and his abstruse meditations resumed. With the assistance of his menials he was at length inserted into cloth garments of a style Mein Herr only can admire. Business occupied him for an hour or two, and making or receiving calls a further space, whilst smoking filled up any leisure before noon. Then he dined, generally with a vigorous appetite, off boiled or grilled fish, salt or fresh meat, and a profusion of vegetables, with oil and butter sauces; upon this foundation he poured copious draughts of Hollands or other spirits. As soon as his plate was removed he returned to his pipe, or napped. At three his slave handed him a cup of tea or coffee, and again made him tidy; with more visits, hearing, transporting, or manufacturing scandal, he at length found his way to nine o'clock, when, as if famished, he paid his respects to a meal of precisely the same heavy character as his dinner. Supper over, and pipe smoked, he now sought a night's rest after such distressing mental and bodily exertion.

The unmarried Dutch lady was extremely careful of her personal appearance. Her dress somewhat resembled that of our Queen Elizabeth. Stiff stays, very long waist, and enormous skirts, in the expansion of which hoops were always employed; her hair was worn either loose or gathered up in a huge knot at the back of the head, and transfixed with two heavy pins, or ornamented with flowers. After marriage she sometimes forgot her careful and cleanly habits, adopted the native fashion of cracking the joints and rubbing them over with oil to make them supple, and acquired a taste for betel and its various concomitants. Whilst scrupulously careful in keeping the reception room clean and orderly, she often allowed the inner apartments to remain in a most miserable, if not disgusting state. She received little attention from her husband, less from her children, the management and castigation of her female slaves occupied the greater part of her time, and ceremonious visits the remainder. The Officials, by keeping themselves very exclusive, retained the good manners of their nation, and transmitted them to their descendants, but their influence was insufficient to counteract the growing vulgarities and degeneracy. It is not, therefore, to be wondered at, that the Dutch lost their possessions in the East; the climate, assisted most materially by their indulgence in heavy food and powerful stimulants, showed their innate laziness of character to perfection, whilst their tolerance of slavery induced such uncharitable feelings towards their dark neighbours as must have procured their expulsion from the Continent had no European rivals appeared.

The English, from a little factory in Surat, had extended their influence during the seventeenth and eighteenth centuries along the coast of India; established the presidencies of Bengal, Bombay, and Madras; foot by foot dispossessed their Portuguese, Dutch, and

French rivals, captured Ceylon in 1782, and taking advantage of the subjection of Holland by the French Republicans, at length appeared, on the 19th October 1795, before Cochin. The expedition, consisting of a detachment of H. M. 77th Regiment, and some Company's troops, under the command of Major Petree, does not appear to have been of any great strength, but the Governor of Cochin was not in a position to emulate its former defence by the Portuguese. A shell was cast with excellent skill into the centre of the Governor's house, bursting, however, without any disaster; the white flag was at once hoisted, and suspension of hostilities agreed to during negotiations for the surrender. The Governor declared his willingness to evacuate the fort on condition that the garrison should, with arms and baggage, and any or all of the inhabitants, be transported in British vessels, and at the British expense, to Batavia; that such of the inhabitants as remained behind should be granted the protection of the British flag; that private property should be respected; that all public documents should be left in his charge; that the fortifications and public buildings should be unmolested; that a free exercise should be granted to all creeds; and that any English deserters found in the town should be pardoned. Major Petree would not bind himself by these stipulations, but demanded that the garrison should surrender its arms and be considered prisoners of war; that the transportation of the inhabitants to Batavia, and the maintenance of the public works, should be dependent on the Honorable Company's orders; and that no promise should be expected in favor of deserters. The Governor, allowed four hours to consider this ultimatum, called together his council at the dead of night, and comparing the strength of the defences with that of the invaders, was inevitably compelled to agree to it. The following morning, the 20th October, the English entered Cochin. The Dutch garrison and some of the inhabitants were eventually transported to Batavia; the cathedral, several of the public buildings, and the whole of the fortifications, were destroyed; and by the peace of 1814 the English were confirmed in their possession of Cochin, Ceylon, Cape Colony, &c., surrendering to the Dutch, Java, Sumatra, and other most valuable islands in the Indian Archipelago.

Thus, Cochin, the scene of the first settlement of Europeans in India, has, after witnessing the last struggles of two great nations, fallen into the possession of the English. How long, and under what circumstances they will hold it, it is impossible to conjecture. Destitute of any defence besides a battalion of native infantry, it might any day be destroyed by an invisible enemy, in steel-plated frigates, armed with Napoleon guns. Considering that besides Bombay we have no harbours of refuge on the Indian coast, and that were the bar at the mouth of the river removed, the harbour of Cochin would offer comfortable room for the whole of our navy, it is strange Government has not thought of increasing the strength of the empire at this point. If any immediate attack were threatened, it is possible more value may be set on Cochin, and that it may yet take an active part in maintaining our astonishing supremacy in India.

BRITISH COCHIN.

CHAPTER II.

DESCRIPTIVE SKETCH.

View from the Roads—The Travancore Backwater—The Harbour—General appearance of the Town—The Cathedral, its great size, and consequent fate—Arrangements of a Dutch house—The Church of St. Francis—The Dutch Cemetery—Parade ground, Garrison—The Sepoy, his pay, promotion and equipment—The Benches—Charming Sunset in the Tropics—Life in Cochin—Wypeen—Its interesting old Church—Dead-house and Burial-ground—Fireworks, gun firing, procession and bell ringing—The Residency.

The view of Cochin and its neighbourhood from the Roads, though probably disappointing to those roseate anticipations of Indian landscape acquired from pictures at home, is by no means uninteresting or devoid of beauty. Before us is the town, embosomed most cosily among tulip, lettuce, and cocoa-nut trees; its venerable Flagstaff Tower and peculiar Church just peeping above the brown tiled roofs of the white and yellow houses. Built on the southern bank of the principal entrance into the Travancore Backwater, it is faced on the north by the island of Wypeen, a low sandy spot densely covered with trees. Looking down this opening inland, we perceive a most extensive lake, the coasts of which are abundantly fertile. North and south, as far as the eye can reach, cocoa-nut plantations succeed each other without a break, rounding wide and narrow bays, or turning sharp peninsulas, and appearing to lessen in size until we lose the line on the horizon. Inland, so far as we can see, stretches a beautifully verdant plain, occasionally relieved by gentle elevations and woody hills; whilst behind, forming a grand termination to so extensive a landscape, are the Southern Ghauts, a noble range of mountains, many apparently of great altitude. The sea is calm and charmingly blue; the air clear and warm, yet fresh; the sky cloudless; and the quiet profound, but for the faint murmur caused by the waves breaking on the bar at the mouth of the river.

Its position at the only navigable entrance into the Backwater has long preserved to Cochin a considerable coast and Arabian trade. This magnificent lagoon, in length about one hundred and seventy, in breadth often twelve miles, runs almost parallel with the sea, and receives the waters of those fast-flowing rivers that rise in the mountains behind, and so excellently irrigate this country. Produce and timber are thus easily conveyed from the most remote spots, industry has always found a vent for its labours, and the population has increased most astonishingly as the demand for the raw staples has improved. The lake we notice just beyond the town is about twelve miles long and five broad; a noble expanse of water, dotted here and there with islands, covered, like the indented shores, with forests of cocoa-nut trees. Remembering that each of these trees is worth one pound sterling when so favourably planted, we may form some idea of the enormous wealth we are so rapidly and comprehensively surveying.

Sir Emerson Tennent, in his most valuable work upon *Ceylon,* thus describes the system of Backwaters which prevails in some portion of that island: "There being no lakes, in the still waters of which the rivers might clear themselves of the earthy matter swept along in their rapid course from the hills, they arrive at the beach laden with sand and alluvium, and at their junction with the ocean being met transversely by the gulf-streams, the sand and soil with which they are laden, instead of being carried out to sea, are heaped up in bars along the shores, and these, being augmented by similar deposits held in suspension by the currents, soon extend to north and south, and force the rivers to flow behind them in search of a new outlet. These formations once commenced, their growth proceeds with rapidity. . . . At the mouth of the rivers, the bars thus created generally follow the direction of the current, and the material deposited being dried and partially consolidated in the intervals between the tides, long embankments are gradually raised, behind which the rivers flow for considerable distances before entering the sea. Occasionally these embouchures become closed by the accumulations without, and the pent-up water assumes the appearance of a still canal, more or less broad according to the level of the beach, and extending for miles along the coast, between the mainland and the new formations. But when swollen by the rains, if not assisted by artificial outlets to escape, they burst new openings for themselves; and not unfrequently they leave their ancient channels converted into shallow lagoons, without any visible exit."

The Backwaters on the Malabar Coast, and the sand or mud bars at their outlets, were doubtless formed in a similar manner.

Passing over the Bar—which is the only interference to this port being, as a harbour of refuge, second to none in India—we enter the broad river. On our right hand is the town, and a more un-oriental-looking place could hardly be conceived. The Flagstaff, erected on the ruined Tower of the Cathedral, is in front; behind is the Cutcherry or Court-house, a painfully white building; around are heavy-looking white, yellow, or grey houses, all tiled, mostly surrounded by high walls, and generally very economical in windows. Here and there in a compound we see the fair green of the Banana, or the dark leaf of the bread-fruit tree; and occasionally we catch a glimpse of a cocoa-nut, which is necessary to remind us of the continent to which we are being introduced. The grass in the open space before us is singularly fresh; surprisingly so in comparison to the burnt up patches of vegetation seen elsewhere in the tropics. Grazing off it in friendly companionship, are white and brown cows, grey and sandy donkeys, mottled and black goats, and long-legged shaggy rusty-coloured sheep. Casks and cases are being dragged on trucks by a choir of coolies, a palankeen is trotting past to the monotonous "hum, hum" of the hamals, and a queer two-wheeled ventilated-bathing-machine-looking carriage and a four-wheeled box-like conveyance are rumbling along the road with all the speed the large-horned white Coimbatore bullocks are capable of. Along the bank are several jetties, erected on cocoa-nut piles, and perhaps a dozen bamboo fishing nets. On the left hand or the

Wypeen side of the river, the broad sandy beach is dotted with miserable little huts, but a few white houses and a large church among the cocoa-nut trees impart some cheerfulness and character to the prospect.

From the platform on the top of the Flagstaff Tower we obtain an excellent idea of the old Dutch houses, their quaint gables, barn-like roofs, heavy walls and buttresses; of the narrow but regular streets; of the venerable Protestant Church, the parade ground beyond it; of the oil yards on the beach and elsewhere, the arrangement of sheds and casks; of the Roads, inner harbour, and country about the extensive Backwater. Coopering appears to be going on in all parts; some produce is being received at one jetty, and a similar kind being shipped at another in capacious cargo boats; the vessels in the inner harbour are rapidly taking in their freight; and an active communication is being held with those outside.

The Tower is a valuable relic of an order of architecture not to be seen in any part of the East but on this coast. With walls at least six feet thick, and strong supporting beams and buttresses, one would imagine it had been erected to resist an apprehended bombardment. The nave, built from east to west, must have covered a large piece of ground, judging from a few traces lately brought to light; and the Dutch showed their appreciation of its spaciousness by making it their principal godown or warehouse, whilst the English, with an eye to a very questionable advantage, soon considered it occupied too large a site, and without any hesitation blew it up. The shock was singularly great, and not only were walls and buildings near this spot riven, but a street of godowns on the parade ground a quarter of a mile off, and the upper story of the present Post-Office—by no means a slight erection—fell in with a crash. The Tower, though seriously injured, stood the shock bravely, and its insolation induced the English to continue the use made of it by the Dutch.

The settlers in any other part of India, with a recollection of their spacious and airy bungalows, their extensive verandahs, and omnipresent venetians, must certainly be tempted to pity the inhabitants of the old Dutch houses in Cochin. A wall ten feet high, and at least two thick, cuts off the house from all vulgar intercourse with the outer world. A narrow gateway, supported on each side by massive pillars, generally adorned with colossal balls, admits us into the compound, or yard; here are some pale roses, scarlet shoe flowers, sweet scented Arabian jessamin, a few bananas, and possibly a choice collection of balsams, marigolds, zinnias, &c., according to the taste of the resident. A flight of fourteen steps leads us to a very small antechamber, dignified—because of the possible admission of a healthy mouthful of air—by the name of verandah. Here we observe two or three lazy chairs, with seducingly wide arms and comfortable wicker backs. A step brings us into a large room, generally divided by a screen into two. The pitch and proportions are good; the ceiling whitewashed; the walls perhaps panelled and relieved by pictures; and light plentiful. The square punkah overhead, the tables, arm chairs, sideboard and bookcase, are truly Dutch; and the taste for quaintly carved clumsy furniture will never be voluntarily improved upon by the cabinet-makers here. In the embrasures of the window two seats are constructed, as is seen in old English mansions. We are naturally surprised to find glass in the windows, and also shutters outside; but remembering the singular delight the Dutchman felt in being snug, we must allow that in this hot climate he very effectually gratified himself. Before the porch and windows are large tatties, or bamboo mats stretched across wooden frames, to keep off the glare of the sun. To the arrangement of the furniture, and not to the elegance in construction of the bed-rooms, any comfort must be attributed, for it is a singular fact that the walls in these old houses are hardly ever parallel to one another, and no regard for uniformity is to be traced in any two doors or windows. The kitchen, usually some five or six yards from the house, is a very unpretending place. The light of the sun peeps through the tiles and the large hole left in the roof for the exit of the smoke, and enables us to see what are the arrangements for cooking. About a dozen open fire places, rudely built with a few bricks, extend along a stone platform; on some of them, kettles and saucepans are delightfully simmering, whilst the cook ladles the brew constantly, and feeds the fires with pieces of wood. At the end of the shed—for it is no better—is a boy squatting beside a blazing wood fire, and turning a spit thrust through an unfortunate fowl, raising the rod on little steps to suit the blaze, and adding fuel from a heap behind him. At night, when the ruddy and uncertain light plays on the dark fellows at work, and illumines many a dark corner and crevice in the old wall, the effect is remarkable. Turkeys, geese, fowls, cats, and dogs, superintend everything from day-light to sunset; but the master and mistress of the house, if anxious to retain a taste for their food, must never make a second visit to this out-station; for, with most limited resources at hand, the cooks are prone to employ very natural although highly objectionable methods in their operations.

It may be conceived that a street of such quaint houses, some painted white, others pale blue, others yellow, and others of no imaginable colour whatever, with no two together exactly alike, with seats at the door of one, columnar sections all over the frontage of another, and colossal balls everywhere, that such a street is picturesque, and, for the tropics, peculiar. With so many strong lights and shades, photographs of this old place come out excellently, the only objection being that they give an excellent idea of a city in Holland immediately after a snow storm, instead of a place but ten degrees from the equator.

The date of the erection of the Church of St. Francis, now called the "Protestant Church," is not known; but from inscriptions still legible on the pavement, we find it existed before 1546, and knowing for a fact that Vasco de Gama in 1525 was interred in the Chancel of the Church of the Franciscans, it may very reasonably be presumed that this is the actual site of his temporary resting place. This is doubtless the oldest European Church in India, and very possibly the most venerable relic of Portuguese power to be seen out of Europe. Until the Dutch captured Cochin, the Roman Catholic form of worship was conducted in its spacious nave with all possible pomp and glitter; but as soon as that clear-headed people entered, the walls were cleared of saints and relics, and a large screen at the end of the Chancel broken down, and threatened with destruction, had it not been for the Wypeen inhabitants, who obtained permission to take it away, and rebuild it in their church over the water.

After the Calvinist forms had been unostentatiously kept up for one hundred and thirty years, the old Church fell into the hands of the English, and owing to its large size, was exposed to the fate that had befallen the Cathedral. Some barrels of gunpowder had been already placed inside, and everything was ready for its demolition, when at the eleventh hour, the officer in command relented, and happily, this interesting pile has no trace of our sad levelling principles.

The Church cannot lay claim to any great architectural merit. It has a tall gable towards the west, with arched windows and porch, columns and pinnacles of a very obsolete fashion. The exterior is more or less blackened by wind and storm. Buttresses, six feet square at the base, support the walls, which are four feet thick. The nave, a hundred and forty-two feet long, fifty-one broad, and to the angle in the strongly braced roof above, fifty high, is airy, bright, and simple; long benches are arranged right and left of the reading desk and pulpit; the stone pavement is occasionally irregular from the deep carvings on some monumental slabs. A broad-spanned arch separates the nave from the Chancel, extending across which, behind the communion table, is a handsomely carved screen with tablets, gold on blue, let into alternate panels. Though the interior is nearly as innocent of ornament as that of a Methodist chapel, its historic interest has made the inhabitants of Cochin highly proud of their old Church.

Many of the inscriptions on the tombs are interesting for their quaint yet characteristic style.

This is a translation of one of the oldest:

"Here lies Maria Memdes, who begs, for the love of God, "one Pater Noster for her soul, died on the 14th October of "the Era 1562 anno."

This is inscribed over a sailor:

"Here rests the old trading Captain Baren Hermans, being "son of Uchtman Haftencer. Deserves for praise a crown. "Vixit 63 years, obiit 29th April, Anno 1673."

The two following are singularly precise:

"Here rests Mistress Lea Vander Koute, wife of the Honorable "Herr Commander Isaac Van-Dielen, died the 29th December, "Anno 1688, being aged thirty-two years, minns a few hours. "And Lea Gertrnda Van-Dielen, little daughter of both, died "11th November previous, aged three years, five months and "seventeen days."

"Here under rests the Honorable Herr Isaac Van-Dielen, Com- "mander and Chief Officer on the Coast of Malabar, Canara, and "Vingorla. Died 25th December, in the evening, between 10 and "11 o'clock, being aged forty-one years, seven months and twenty "days, Anno 1693."

And this appears to be the most recent:

"Here under rests, for holy Resurrection, the body of the de- "ceased, well born, Herr Reinen Van-Harm, in life Senior "Merchant, Second,* and Head Administrator of this Govern- "ment. Born at Campen on the 12th December 1734. Died the "16th March 1789, aged fifty-four years, three months and four "days."

Since 1794 burials have not taken place in the Church, the vaults were filled up, and the doors seldom unlocked, until, in 1817, the Bishop of Calcutta appointed a clergyman to this coast, and after a long period of but monthly services, the present Chaplain was established to this

* *i.e.*—Second in rank to the Governor General of Batavia.

town individually by the Additional Clergy Society. His comfortable Parsonage, close by, is surrounded by a large garden, containing a rare collection of tropical fruits and flowers.

Near to the Church is the old Dutch Cemetery, a small square plot enclosed within high walls. The tombs, flat, dome, and pyramidically shaped, are occasionally diversified by broken pillars, urns, and sarcophagi, all more or less blackened by exposure; the grass rank and wild, here and there lost sight of among bushes of a beautiiul orange-flowered weed that infests this part of India. The new Burial Ground is a mile and a half distant from the town.

The Parade Ground occupies the heart of the town beyond the Church. The Hospital, Guard House, and Magazine are situated on one side under the shade of large tulip and bread-fruit trees; and around, beyond the road, are some commodious houses, among which, at the right-hand corner, are the Telegraph and Post Offices. The grass, delightfully green, has not yet overgrown some traces of the godowns alluded to in a preceding page, and no one has cause to regret the clcarance so singularly effected.

The town is garrisoned by a detachment of H.M. 45th Regiment M. N. I., consisting of one European Captain aud one European Lieutenant, one Subadar Major, corresponding in rank to a Captain, one ordinary Subadar or Lieutenant, two Jemadars or Ensigns, ten Havildars or Sergeants, ten Naiques or Corporals, two Drummers, and a hundred and fifty Privates. The Barracks, or Sepoy Lines, are about a quarter of a mile from the town, among cocoa-nut and bamboo trees.

It is probable that this small military force will have been relieved by a body of native police before the publication of this volume. The extraordinary measures now pursued by the Viceregal Government to raise from the ashes of Sepoy rascality a *native police* who shall do its duty *honestly*, naturally excite much alarm among all classes in India, for perhaps in no other part of the world are men so easily tempted to corrupt practices as hère. The Sepoy seldom possessed such opportunities to defeat the ends of justice as are now necessarily afforded the policeman, or we should have heard of great domestic iniquity on every side. Moreover, to the latter is given such authority over Europeans as is only too likely to be exercised for personal motives, for a native is never so much pleased as when he may snub or domineer over a sahib. The sahib, as a rule, cannot put up with insolence, and despite the terrors of the cutcherry chastises the native, and incurs the penalty for so doing. It is all very well for Viceroys and Members of Council to attempt to legislate against such difficulties, by disarming, fineing, and imprisoning the sahib, when he practically evinces his opposition to native control; but they forget that he, if an ordinary personage, does not experience the servile obedience which they receive from every man. To witness a herd of native officials dragging along, cruelly cuffing, and cowardly kicking some European delinquent, is enough to tempt any proper man to forget himself; for when he does not blindly charge into the rascals, he commences with expostulation, receives some insolent reply, and then, as a matter of course, knocks the belted peon over; for which offence the magistrate has to punish him severely, a result that usually gives great satisfaction to every native present, and induces further quarrels. It is too much to expect that the native policeman shall prove himself beyond the temptation of a bribe, and of exercising his authority maliciously when brought in contact with an European; and it is yet more absurd to look for such deference by the European to power held by a native as would be exhibited if it were invested in a fellow-countryman.

The Sepoy, voluntarily enlisted, receives from seven to nine rupees a month, according to his conduct and term of service; and at the end of fifteen years can claim a pension of about four rupees per mensem. But promotion being solely influenced by seniority, he may always hope to receive a commission before that time, and be thereby entitled on his retirement to a more considerable income. In proportion to what he could earn in any civil occupation, the pay is liberal; yet he is mostly a discontented mortal, always grumbling about *batta*, high prices of provisions, &c. The system of promotion is open to objection; for as every private may be said to have a captain's commission in his knapsack, the native officer receives very little respect from the men off parade; and the injustice shown to ability naturally hinders its appearance. His dress may be martial, but it most certainly is not picturesque. A high glazed leather head-piece, resembling a coal-scuttle in shape, a scarlet cloth tail coat, black cloth trowsers (except on show days, when white cotton are worn), and leather sandals, complete the costume of an unfortunate being who, off duty, is well contented with a piece of cotton cloth round his waist. The reflection of the rays of a tropical sun from the helmet and scarlet coat is almost intolerable; what then must be the discomfort of a native so singularly clothed! The Turco or Zouave in his fez cap, open jacket, wide breeches, and yellow leather gaiters, might for once indulge in a sentiment of pity were he to be introduced to one of H.M. Madras Native Infantry.

Some interesting relics of the old rampart are to be seen around the Fort. A short promenade has been made of a portion of the beach, tulip trees thereon planted, and a few simple benches set up at the corner of the bastion. Here, in the cool of the evening, merchants "much do congregate;" discuss any news, and lay down most excellent laws for "how to do it." A broad sandy beach, about two miles long, and a boundless expanse of water, stretches out in front; the breeze is soft and refreshing after the hot day, and the sunset generally glorious. The sky seems washed with fire, the clouds tinted with virgin gold, and their fleecy folds embathed in regal purple; the east reflects the brilliance among the lights and shades of the rising vapours, and at length the lingering light decays, the sea relinquishes its borrowed splendour, and the sun suddenly sinks beneath the horizon. These tropical sunsets are magnificent, and their charms further enhanced by the sweet murmuring of

> "the bridegroom sea,
> As he toys with the shore his wedded bride,
> And in the fulness of his marriage joy
> Decorates her tawny brow with shells,
> Retires a space to see how fair she looks,
> Then, proud, runs up to kiss her."

Cochin does not thoroughly awake until six in the morning: then the crows summon a parliament; shutters are unfastened; doors opened; goats and cows trot out; fishermen set busily to work; water boys, tappal men, and telegraph peons chase one another; yard bells begin to ring; operatives assemble; trucks and carts soon issue out; coolies throng the streets; sahibs, some on foot, some on horseback, some in bandies, at length reach their offices; and activity reigns around. At noon, dinner causes a slight lull; at five the day's work is over. Then the inhabitants take exercise: ladies, attired in wide-awakes, natty white jackets and black cloth skirts, and gentlemen in costume much resembling that of painters, are seen mounted on cream-coloured, chestnut, or white ponies; and easy-going pedestrians, quasi crinoline, babies, ayahs, peons, and bandies, enliven the promenade. Night falls: shutters are bolted; gates barred; and before eight o'clock the town seems wrapped in slumber, except when some warm-hearted neighbour has invited his friends to a dance, and engaged the services of the Cochin band, which, with or without permission, is generally successful in keeping the neighbourhood awake till three or four in the morning, at which time the National Anthem, vigorously accompanied on fife, violin, and big drum, is chanted by the excited guests with most stunning pathos. The celebration of the nuptials of the Portuguese is sometimes kept up uninterruptedly from nine in the morning of one day to three in the night of the day following, that is, for more than forty hours. In olden times dancing parties were of yet longer duration in this quaint old place; the day time being mostly passed in singing, flirting, and luxurious feeding, and the night in vigorous dancing. A little before six on Sunday morning the Church bell is rung to remind the inhabitants of the day; the quiet of a country village in England is maintained, and Jew, Mohammedan, and Hindoo, abstain from all important work.

Crossing the Inner Harbour we land at Wypeen, and obtain another view of the little Fort. The number of fishing nets on both sides of the river is surprising; and as they appear, for half the day at least, slowly moving into and out of the water, and generally enclose a goodly quantity of fish every five minutes, some curiosity is excited to know what becomes of it all. There are also several men ferrying about with paddles in small canoes, warily drawing in and letting out long lines, until at last a fine salmon-like fellow is drawn out writhing most fiercely, and thrown into the bottom of the boat. By the time the shore is reached the fish is dead, and in a prime condition for the dissection that at once commences on the bank. The flesh is very like turbot.

There is an interesting Roman Catholic Church here. Its quaint mediæval roof, white walls, square and twisted pillars and undecorated windows, seem incongruous beside the cocoa-nut, bread-fruit, and banana trees. At some distance in front of the door is a large hexagonal building of the same style of architecture, with a cupola surmounted by a high wooden cross. On the right hand is the Dead-house, a dark damp place, with an altar and some old granite slabs inside. A little Burial-ground behind seems too small for the purpose, as in a pit at the corner are a number of bones, that have been, not wantonly, but apparently by necessity, exhumed, to give room for other occupants of the poor sandy soil. By buying the ground out and out, and erecting a tomb or railing around the plot, this desecration does not extend to the dust of those whose friends are rich; otherwise, as a rule in Indian cemeteries, no respect is paid to a grave after three or four years. In a Chapel close by, behind a glass case, is a miserable little piece of wood carved into something resembling a man, clothed in what was once black silk velvet, and declared to be a portraiture of Saint Maurice; day and night poor black women come in, cross themselves, kiss their fingers most reverentially, touch the glass, hold out their little babies to touch it also, and then depart. It is a pitiful sight to witness.

Behind the high altar of the Church is the screen which originally occupied the end of the chancel of the Protestant Church. It is divided by pairs of fluted columns into six compartments, two of which are occupied by gaudy effigies of the Virgin. The two below to the right and left contain paintings of St. Beneventuro and St. Francis, probably executed in Europe more than three hundred years ago; above them are native designs of St. Joseph and St. Dominique, and though the colours may be slightly discordant, and the perspective enough to throw a Turner into convulsions, we must certainly admit the attempts are praiseworthy. On the right and left of the nave is a highly painted altar piece, the former containing an effigy of the Mother and Child, surmounted by a glory, and the latter a representation of the Crucifixion, which from the knowledge of anatomy exhibited must have had an European origin. The pulpit, resembling a sacramental goblet in design, is decorated in alto-relievo, with figures of five saints, and covered by a rather elegantly shaped canopy. Nothing is, however, so striking as the perfect indifference manifested for harmony in colours. A scarlet and ochre pulpit, dull red rails across the nave, greenish blue altar pieces, and highly-tinted mouldings, cannot be considered good taste; but such pre-Raphaelitism is not confined to Cochin.

On the eve of feast days the interior of this and other similar Churches in the district are illuminated with small oil lamps ; minute guns are fired outside ; rockets, blue and red fires, most lavishly expended ; and torchlight processions perambulate the highways with kettledrum, tom-tom, trumpet, and fife, uniting in grand uproar. The Hindoos have very similar ceremonies, so the din raised out of the fort till late at night is sometimes most annoying to poor sleepless Protestants, as the Roman Catholics seem to employ the greater part of time in recording its progress, and bells are almost always ringing, whether for service or not no one seems to know or care. There is a solemn-voiced bell at the other end of Wypeen, behind the çocoa-nut trees, and at night, when all else is still, the sound comes in detachments on the breeze, so gently and so modestly, that breathing is momentarily suspended to enjoy its sweetness more entirely.

By far the larger portion of the inhabitants of British Cochin are Roman Catholics. Their bigotry is something approaching to the ludicrous, and their devotion to the "cloth" to idolatry. The priests are, with a few exceptions, under-educated, conceited, small-minded men, such as are the pest of a town like this, and are the obstacles to the introduction of salutary reforms. Excommunication and penance are frequently sentences for the most trifling opposition to the priestly will, and an inquisitorial confession required, that, it has been proved, has sometimes been shamefully directed to immoral purposes. The flock is not allowed to think, read, or act for itself; it is trained from childhood to feel the utmost reverence for its pastor's judgment, and consequently all attempts to Protestantize individuals have failed. Business is frequently much delayed by the occurrence of saints' days, festivals, and fasts, and no amount of opposition has yet overcome the interruption. The writers, coopers, carpenters, and coolies, take these holidays as a matter of course, and the employer has simply to make his people work extra the day before and the day after. Again, a sort of idea seems to prevail that Cochin is the centre of civilization, the modern Cadiz, after seeing which nothing remains in the world worth beholding. Generations of the Portuguese and Dutch descendants consequently remain within the precincts of the town during their whole lives; and never does any desire seem to arise to investigate the neighbourhood even; except when ordered away, they spend a holiday in macadamising the roads in the town in preference to learning something of the treasures so illimitably, so temptingly, so maturedly displayed in this gorgeously carpeted land.

At about a mile and a half from the fort, upon an island in the large lake, is the Residency, a good type of the modern Bungalow. The rooms, spacious and well furnished, open into a large and airy verandah, whence the view between the trees and over the grand sheets of water is most agreeable. The grounds are planted with a variety of noble trees, the grass is well cropped and green, and the place otherwise much resembles a snug corner in a finely wooded park at home.

NATIVE COCHIN.

CHAPTER III.

THE BAZAAR.

Character of the Town around the Fort—False ideas in connexion with a Bazaar—That at Cairo very interesting—Those in Cochin inferior—Paticnce of dealers — Dispute in bargaining—Money-changer—Jeweller—Opium dealer—Curry shop—Coppersmith—Box-maker—Mercer—Herbalist—Lace-maker—Hawkers of fisb, poultry, confectionery, &c.—Village trade—Market women—Butcher—Baker—Poulterer—Dhoby—Tailor.

It would be difficult to describe the arrangement of that part of the Cochin metropolis in which are to be found the dwellings of the hundreds of operatives who earn their livelihood in the Fort as coopers, carpenters, ironmongers, sawyers, &c., for it extends more or less among the plantations around, sometimes as a collection of small villages, at others scattered without any regard to neighbourhood. There are few main roads, but in their place a number of winding paths, generally low and damp like the ground on which the huts are erected; and as the plantations are seldom enclosed, a short cut can be made in any direction with some little knowledge of the locality of the evergreen ponds, canals, and paddy fields which so richly irrigate the district, at the expense, it is to be feared, of the natives' health. From the north-east corner of the Fort two good roads proceed, one into the Cochin, the other into the Travancore territory. The latter is almost entirely overhung by cocoa-nut and banian trees, and forms an agreeable ride; there are few shops, all of the most ordinary character, and little to remark either in wares, dealers, or customers; but the other road, towards the Rajah's palace, is enlivened for nearly two miles by the presence on either side of shops and stores, and the scene generally animated in the extreme.

It is not agreeable to have to divest oneself of a fancy that in younger days, and even in mature life, may have been productive of many a romantic and indescribably pleasant idea; and this cannot be better exemplified than in connexion with a *Bazaar*. At home we associate it with a gay and costly assortment of wares, temptingly arranged before charming demoiselles, whose ringlets and smiles ensure brisk trade. Then we read, when children, of bazaars in Persia and elsewhere, where gold, precious stones, and draperies are exposed in such lavish profusion, and under such bustling and gay auspices, that one is inclined to imagine that "if there *is* a heaven on earth, it is *there!* it is *there!*" Then we have all studied in the "Arabian Nights," of how that King of Caliphs, Haroun Alraschid, walked through the streets of his capital incognito, and listened to what people said concerning him and his rule. And who has not felt deep respect for the good, the sagacious, the venerable Vizier, by whose courteous behaviour to the storekeepers we are introduced with the observant Caliph into back chambers, and there permitted to see caskets of precious stones, statues of pure gold, and boxes of costly garments? Who, then, does not associate the bazaar with all things luxurious and beautiful? That at Cairo is certainly worth attention. In the open shops are grand displays of shawls, jewels, and trinkets; the air is occasionally perfumed with the sweetest of oriental scents, as a dealer opens a bottle for the judgment of a customer; and the streets are mostly thronged with camels, horses, mules, gilded chariots, screaming runners, and hawkers shouting out the superlatively excellent qualities of their wares. Upon the richly caparisoned mules are ladies of the harem, attired in the most valuable silks and satins; and marching by their side are several tall, thin, fiercely moustached mulattoes. The variety of the costume, from the fez and flowing white tunic of the barber, to the turban, cloth of gold robe, and jewelled scimitar of the Pasha, is most pleasing; and the incessant shaving, coffee drinking, smoking, and gossipping on all sides, with the deafening cries of runners, hawkers, and enthusiastic Britons urging their steeds at full gallop through the throng, are calculated to please a stranger greatly. But there are also such sad cases of ophthalmia, skin diseases, and malformations, and such painful evidences of poverty, wickedness, and misery visible on all sides, that in a few days the glitter and bustle become as distasteful as honey to an alderman's palate. The Cochin bazaars cannot compare with even those in Egypt; but as giving some idea of the tastes, food, and clothing of the natives, it may be well to proceed rapidly through that called the Muttencherry, which runs along the Backwater for some distance.

The houses are generally built upon a small embankment raised two feet above the level of the road. They comprise the shop, open in front like a coach-house, a back store-room, and two or three small rooms in the floor above. The dealer squats in the centre of his wares, and waits for customers with truly exemplary patience. At length one arrives, and he takes care that it shall be his fault if there is any silence in the market for five minutes at least. By that time the purchaser may be satisfied, and takes away the dispute with his investment. The method of barter employed by the natives seems to be one of *banter* on the part of both buyer and seller, together with a lavish supply of falsehoods and impudent personalities; and the consequence is that a vast amount of time is lost in the squabble before an arrangement is concluded. In offering produce to an European, the native, with the most bland assurance, lies mightily as a preface, and then names some extravagant price for the article, which is promptly met by an offer of one-half, or less. Pity at the ignorance of the European, not unmixed with offended dignity at having the offer thus practically dealt with, is inimitably portrayed, and perhaps he moves off, and, after declaring elsewhere that the offer made to him was such as he had proposed, he returns, and finally accepts a reasonable figure. By the expert use of this system he plucks the *griffin* most cruelly; but also sells him experience which soon defeats the game.

The variety of trades is remarkable. Here is a money-changer, who will give chuckrums or annas for rupees, and pocket four to six per cent. by the exchange; or he will buy up foreign gold and silver at a rate which is not complimentary to the august head on the coins, except it be that of an English sovereign, and especially one stamped with St. George and the Dragon on the reverse, and for these (which are in request as ornaments) he will pay the equivalent of twenty-one shillings to even twenty-two shillings value. English gold is generally at a premium since the natives have been convinced of its comparative purity; and large amounts are supposed to be now buried in various parts of the country, and may never be recovered, as the proprietors frequently die without pointing out the treasure. The Australian sovereign is with difficulty sold at par; it looks too bright, lacks the royal arms, and also the advantage of good minting. The next shop is that of a jeweller, an old lynx-eyed Mussulman, engaged most intently in engraving some silver work. He appears to have no stock in trade besides two or three sharp-pointed instruments, a little stage to work on, and a small stone hand-wheel; but get that old gentleman to conceive you are a likely purchaser, and he produces from some hidden retreat a variety of beautiful silver wire brooches, bracelets, and hair pins, of such workmanship as no European could equal, excepting, perhaps, the iron wire-maker of Berlin. Next comes an opium dealer, a healthy fair-coloured Brahmin, with anything but the lack-lustre eye and emasculated body of the consumer of his nation-destroying wares. The article is sold in any quantity, at a price which fortunately does not bring it within the reach of the operative class. It is a dark glossy brown substance, with the strong disagreeable odour of poppies, and a bitter sickening taste which remains long in the mouth. Next is a curry-stuff shop. Here arranged in baskets on shelves by the side and before the dealer are grains, coriander, popperdum, ulva, and cummin seeds, green and dry ginger, black and white pepper, green and scarlet chillies, tamarinds, almonds, turmeric, and a number of other roots, fruits, and seeds. The fragrance of the spices is very strong, and helps in a great measure to season the atmosphere of the vicinity. Next is a rice shop, where grain of many qualities is exposed in husk, clean or boiled. Next is a coppersmith's. Here a large vessel is being hammered into shape with such stunning noise and persevering activity as must make nerves at a premium in the neighbourhood. Several very strongly wrought and highly-burnished brass pots, vases, basins, and lamps, are exposed in front for sale, side by side, occasionally with some monstrosity, which, after the Priest's dedication, will be set up in the owner's house and worshipped. Next a box maker's. Here are several men engaged at work, some putting in locks and hinges, and others fastening on brass corners and bindings; to the profusion of which, and not to the security of the box, the native directs his *first* attention. A study of the locks, though it might fail to furnish Mr. Hobbs with a new idea, ought certainly to amuse that inventor; for the object in their manufacture can certainly not be that to which he is accustomed. As the native seldom has more clothes than he could conveniently hold in one hand, and rarely possesses books or other large and heavy articles, one small box is all the accommodation that he at any time is likely to require, and even in this he is never induced to lock up his money, but prefers carrying it about on his person, or burying it under his house. Next is a mercer's. Here, piled up to the roof, are parcels of silk and cotton cloths for men and women, coarse red cotton handkerchiefs, muslins of different hues and textures, and a small quantity of English broadcloth. Next is the herbalist's. Hanging from the roof, around, before, and behind the dealer, are bundles of dry roots and herbs. These are sold readily to the natives, who have a considerable knowledge of the medicinal qualities of each, and often administer them with such results as have been vainly expected from the best European drugs. As in more civilized countries, the women are most fertile in resources for many sicknesses, sprains, and contusions, but the men also are well acquainted with the properties of each medicine, and the children acquire orally such information about the treatment of slight ills as not one Englishman in twenty possesses, fortunately for the doctor. Next is a lace-maker's. Here three or four women are squatting before square pillows, handling the gold and silk thread, and letting in bright beads with a dexterity such as might make a Honiton lassie blush. Their hands are very small, their fingers thin and flexible, and they are most skilful copyists, but working out an original design, or even doing more than ribbon or finger lace without some superintendence is quite out of their power. They work with smaller pins, but on larger pillows than are seen in England and Belgium. Sleeve embroidery has lately been introduced into the country, and the women are eminently successful in this branch of needlework; though the time occupied in the manufacture is tedious, even in comparison to the progress of young ladies at home in similar undertakings, with a pleasant companion on one side, and the latest novel on the other.*

* Since the above was written the rage for embroidery has gradually ceased in England, sane people having begun to see the frivolity of the labour. Far better return to the employments of our foremothers, and cover our walls with artistic tapestry, than revive a fashion which induced a cessation of useful, nay necessary, needlework, for the sake

Then there are, in the street, fruiterers, poulterers, confectioners, and hawkers of various kinds of shrimps, anchovies, herrings, mullets, &c., the odour of which under the hot sun is horrible! most horrible! A number of women selling milk, butter, and butter-milk, in little pouches made ont of leaves; and vendors of nasty-looking sweetmeats, made of rice, sugar, &c., baked in rings, sticks, and crosses, to suit the fancy; together with circular cakes of jagghery, a coarse sugar obtained from the cocoa-nut tree. After these, dealers in vegetables, great yams, some small as new potatoes, others as large as an elephant's foot; bananas, green, yellow, and blackish, small and large, either for eating raw or curried; cocoa-nuts, whole, or opened and divided into sections, and many other things; then sellers of eggs, sugar cane, popperdums,* betel leaf, areca nut, salt, lime, and such miscellaneous articles as lobsters' claws (used as graters), grass brooms, wicker-work stools, earthen pots, skeins of cotton, thread and coir yarn, teak leaves for wrapping up curry, split bamboos for making hedges, cadjans for thatching huts, and cart loads of banana leaves, which are used as plates throughout India, from the poor deformed beggar to the Rajah on the musnud.

The Bazaar is generally crowded with people, many carrying high parcels of yarn, leaves, and bamboos, or baskets of grain, lime, and fruit; some bargaining with

of the hem of a petticoat, and thereby strengthen that taste for display which unhappily characterises the attire of *all* classes now-a-days.

* Popperdums are thin white cakes, made of small grain, pounded very fine, and beaten into a paste with a solution of water, salt, and "popperdo-karom," a species of sandy mineral. When fried they impart an agreeable and wholesome relish to curry. Large quantities are exported yearly to Bombay, Colombo, and elsewhere.

dealers; and others more intent upon something further on, pushing their way rapidly through the throng. As the majority of the men have nothing on but a piece of cloth round the waist, and the costume of the women differs but slightly on market days, it may be conceived that the evaporation from such a crowd is disagreeable in the highest degree, and especially so when as many as can afford it rub cocoa-nut oil into their tawny skins till they shine again. Cows wander about listlessly, picking up a fallen leaf or fruit, and treating themselves to a mouthful of grain from a basket in a shop when the owners' eyes are directed elsewhere. Their holy character in the eyes of all good Hindoos preserves them from ill-treatment for getting in the way, a number of women follow them assiduously to collect their dung (for purposes mentioned in the next chapter), and the road is thus kept clear at all times of a nuisance. Goats are to be seen in the wake of the cows, with a troop of black and white kids bleating around them, and though not protected by any alleged sanctity of character, it is a rare thing to see a native raise his hand against them. The pretty little kids are often much worried by the cowardly pariah dogs that abound in the market. These animals are mostly of a light tan color, with a fox-like head and cunning eyes, and are generally as large as beagles, but nothing like so plump in build. They snarl and howl in a manner truly horrible, and are entirely devoid of the fine characteristics of the British dog, worrying all weaker animals with a maliciousness that might be expected from their cringing bearing towards man. In every store some poor lean white cat may be seen, of a race as degenerate as that of the dog, and possessing a "mew," to which the plaint of the "old tom cat on the tiles so flat" at home is harmonious in comparison. Large raven-like crows infest the neighbourhood, and pick up odd scraps and garbage with an audacity truly remarkable. They are not particular in their diet, but seem to act upon the American Indian's principle of stuffing the stomach with red clay to fill up the vacuum when more savoury edibles are scarce; and it is a blessing in the tropics that these birds are so hungry and omnivorous, for otherwise a plague would soon be generated by the exhalations of their disgusting food. There is hardly any lull in the uproar during the day, with men shouting, women screeching, and crows cawing; but as evening approaches the crowd thins; the shops are bolted up, or the goods taken into an apartment in the rear and stored away; and the dealers betake themselves to the upper story, or to some little snuggery in the compound behind. Hardly a sound disturbs the stillness of the night in the Bazaar, excepting when some poor diseased outcast slinks under the shelter of the overhanging thatch of a shop, places his staff at his side, twists himself into the smallest possible compass, wraps his dirty cloth tightly around him, and speedily falls asleep, proving that

> " 'tis not only on downy couch
> Or 'neath the shade of lofty canopy that sleep is found."

The Bazaars are supplied twice or thrice a week with fresh provisions, &c.; and the natives from the interior come regularly at those periods to make such purchases as will suffice for a few days. From the inland market food is taken to provide a yet more distant village, and the same article often travels about from place to place until it gets stale and bad. Women are generally employed to transport the supply, and labour as assiduously as their sisters in Covent-garden; but here the resemblance ceases; for whilst they are poor, melancholy, prematurely aged persons, bending beneath the weight of insipid fruits, the latter are fine strapping country-women, engaged in arranging vegetables of such fresh color, with violets of such perfume, as cannot be imagined in the Indian Bazaar. Associated, doubtless, with the unclad condition of all around, there is an air of gnawing hunger in the eagerness of barter that is quite miserable to see; and though necessities of life here are few, the difficulty of satisfying them appears extreme. There is indeed much of novelty to remark in the Indian Bazaar, but it is of that character which successfully materialises the imagination, and forces us most unwillingly to be sceptical upon descriptions in the "Arabian Nights."

The European inhabitants of the Fort are dependent upon the Bazaar chiefly for the necessaries of life, and to such an extent as is sometimes painfully annoying. An enterprising Hindoo has monopolised the meat trade for several years, and retained his advantage by buying out rivals, and rapidly raising prices afterwards to reimburse the outlay. His shop is extremely simple, constructed of bamboos, plaited cocoa-nut leaves, and plastered with cow-dung. A block about two feet high occupies the centre of the hovel, sitting before which, with his legs conveniently stretched on either side, the Butcher of Cochin may generally be seen mangling the mortal remains of, it may be, some naturally defunct quadruped; whilst patiently standing before him are the servants from the various houses in the town. The oxen of this part of the world are too valuable as beasts of draught to permit their slaughter for table purposes, and consequently cows which, either from an unsanguine temperament or from old age, have ceased to give lactescent returns, are killed, and their various parts distributed in every direction. The cow beef is often obtained from the jungles, and then indeed one requires

> "the keen dispatch
> Of real hunger and concoctive heat
> To transubstantiate it."

But generally the meat turns out more tender than might be expected from the aspect of the raw material. Paulghaut supplies the town with long-legged rusty-fleeced sheep, and these are economically slain to suit the demand. The flesh is sometimes very excellent; mint and spicy ingredients are not wanting to make it more palatable; and travellers have been heard to declare that better mutton is not obtainable in India, nor even at Capel Curig in North Wales. Pigs are reared successfully round every cottage where rice is eaten, and rice-bran necessarily abundant; but the fattest are to be found in the vicinity of the cocoa-nut-oil mills, as the *poonac* or oil-cake is almost invariably thrown to them. The market value of meat varies considerably; the average prices are for beef 2½*d.*, pork 3¾*d.* per lb.; mutton is sold in pieces—hind-quarter 2*s.* 6*d.*, leg 1*s.* 3*d.*, shoulder or loin 10*d.*, neck 6½*d.*, and breast 8¾*d.* Occasionally the butcher strikes, demands higher rates, and invariably obtains them from all individuals desirous of some variation from duck and curried fowl, and fowl and curried duck. Almost all the natives are vegetarians, and

Europeans are soon instructed by Nature to assimilate their diet somewhat to that indigenous to the district; so the consumption of animal food is never very considerable, and the chance seems small of a Bannister setting up in opposition to the Cochin Chamberlain, and maintaining such an exalted position for any length of time.

There is no want of bakers in the town; indeed the trade is not sufficient to remunerate those now established. The wheat is imported from Bombay, Mangalore, &c., ground very fine in hand-mills, made into bread with toddy yeast, and baked in low brick ovens heated by external fires of the oil-pervading cocoa-nut shell. Bread is generally made in double rolls or half loaves, for which 1½*d.* is charged, but lately some alteration has been effected to suit the demand on festive occasions. Milk is brought round regularly every morning, not in bright metal cans with natty little tins clustering around, but in long black glass bottles that have a wonderful resemblance to those corked by the Friend of India; yet, as it is not agreeable to associate the flavor of hops with milk, it is wise to suppose that these are *not* beer bottles. The price of milk rarely alters from 2 *rs.* per dozen bottles, or about 1*d.* per pint. Butter is brought from distant villages where the demand for milk is poor, and sold at 10*d.* per lb.; but every one who keeps a cow provides himself, as the country manufacture is singularly insipid and oily. Poultry comes from the interior at all seasons of the year in a sadly lean and anxious condition, so that it is necessary to fatten a purchase for weeks before it is fit for the table. For ducks 6*s.*, for fowls 7*s.* per dozen is asked, and for geese and turkeys 2*s.* 6*d.* per pair. The turkeys are large, and the ducks and geese hardly inferior to those at home, but the fowls are weaker, and certainly less interesting than any species reared in a colder climate.* Rice is brought from Bombay, Ceylon, and Calcutta, sometimes in abundant quantities, at others so insufficiently that subscriptions have to be raised to preserve the poor from actual starvation. The curse upon "him that withholdeth corn" is here heard low but deep, and were it not for Protestant assistance the misery would be extreme every monsoon, as charity is a virtue wofully unappreciated by the heathen in this money-hoarding land, and the Roman Catholic contributes so large a proportion of his savings towards fireworks and the illumination of the church, that any benevolent schemes have to be put on the shelf of good intentions. With the certain prospect of many a rainy day at the close of the year, it seems marvellous that the natives do not lay by something when they possess the power; but, unhappily, poor people here are no wiser than their whiter brethren in other countries, and are as little able to comprehend and as unwilling to act upon principles of economy.

Potatoes are brought down from the Neilgherries in bullock bandies or carts, and cost about 1¼*d.* per lb. Coffee (6*d.* per lb.) is well supplied from Allway, Cottayam, and the immediate vicinity of the town. Tea occasionally arrives direct from China in native vessels; green (5*s.* to 6*s.* per lb.) is hardly ever purchased, but

* Individuals—for whom it may be hoped the mystical letters F. G. S. are in store—are firm in maintaining that Cochin China fowls are to be found in Cochin on the Malabar Coast, but no bird of such a singular appearance has as yet been discovered in this part of India.

black (2*s.* 6*d.* to 3*s.* 6*d.* per lb.) is consumed rather largely. Black salt ($\frac{1}{2}$*d.* per lb.) is obtained from Bombay at the end of the monsoon, and cleaned in each house before employment with boiling water and the white of eggs. Sugar (6*d.* per lb.) is imported in as rude a condition from Calcutta, and in small quantities from the interior. Beer, wines, and spirits are brought direct from England and France, but Bombay is also resorted to when supplies are scanty; for in the Bazaar sherry especially suffers from the "cow with the iron tail" principle; and the misery is, that instead of simply diluting it with water, the shopman adds a dose of villainous spirit that makes the mouth smart again; and so people are compelled, in self-preservation, to supply themselves from a distance, and the tradesmen justly enough enjoy but little business in these articles.

The Dhoby is an "institution" as peculiar to India as the Falls of Niagara are to "the States." Men and women are trained up from infancy to adopt this profession of their ancestors, and, dying, cast their mantles on their own offspring by the inevitable law of caste, which confines each trade to a peculiar class. In Cochin the Dhobies are immediately distinguishable by their dark chestnut, if not inkish-hued skin, their small but vigorous frame, and their usually cheerful, self-satisfied, rotund physiognomy. The love of ornament is a mania with them, and indulged even when at work by the oldest as well as the youngest of the women. Silver toe and finger-rings, bracelets, necklaces, and gilded ear-rings are worn in profusion, without any regard for either effect or neighbourhood.

The mode of cleaning linen is somewhat interesting

on first acquaintance, but experience of the mangling tendencies of the process soon induces most uncomplimentary sentiments towards the unfortunate Dhoby. The clothes are taken about once a week in a huge bundle from each house, and sorted at the *laundry* into cottons, muslins, and silks. The cottons are immediately thrown into a boiler, and allowed to soak for half a day or so, and then taken out, rinsed, and carried to the *dhoby-ground*. This is a large open space, about a mile from the town, surrounded by cocoa-nut trees on all sides but one, into which the sea-breeze enters most delightfully. In various parts are stagnant pools, some six, some sixty feet wide, and from one to five feet deep, abundantly productive of great toads, and oppressively redolent of primitive vegetation. Around each of these pools are large flattened pieces of stone, at a distance of from six to a dozen paces from one another, and before these, with their legs semi-immersed in water, the Dhobies continue their work. The articles are taken from a bundle in the serpentine form assumed after rinsing, dipped, and beaten with no mean violence, or sluggish care, upon the stones, whilst occasionally the foot is employed to rub out any peculiarly dark spots. They are now clean, and thus, either on the spot or in the Dhoby's house, are placed in a tub of rice starch, and after another rinse hung out in the sun to dry, which, it may be imagined, the sun is here capable of doing very rapidly. They are now sprinkled with fresh water and ironed. The "*iron*" is made of copper, upon a very simple and intelligent principle. The base is an inch or more high, constructed like a box, with a small lid under the wooden handle, under which is an ample space for a handful of charcoal and pieces of cocoa-nut shells. This fuel burns very slowly when the lid is closed, with the assistance of a little ventilation through holes in the side. Thus the iron—or rather copper—is always hot, so long as the internal fire is kept up, and its temperature can be varied by adding or extracting fuel. Muslins are generally boiled with a little soap made of "popperdokarom," oil, &c., but never beaten on the stones, neither are coloured clothes and silks, which are washed by friction between the hands, as in England. Cow-dung and potash are thrown into the boiler when the clothes are more than ordinarily unclean, but this is only necessary in the purification of the natives' robes.

The dhoby is paid by residents at the rate of nine to ten shillings per mensem for each individual in the family, or enters into a contract for the *house* if the olive branches are tender and numerable. By this arrangement everything has to be washed when wanted, sheets, pillows, curtains, covers, table cloths, handkerchiefs, turbans, and the numberless and nameless articles of male and female, adult and juvenile attire; all are taken in a lump and counted out to the dhoby for return in a week or fortnight. Travellers, or occasional residents, are obliged to pay at about the rate of eight shillings per hundred *pieces,* a piece being either a collar or counterpane, a necktie or nightgown, a towel or turban, all the same. This is a curious system, for increase of labour in preparing an article justifies increase of charge for the work, and doubtless the dhobies think so, and very likely do not quite comprehend why the rates, well enough for making up a native's linen, should be assumed as the standard for remuneration after exercises of patience in submitting to endless abuse from British patrons. Buttons must be broad-cast beneath the waters of the stagnant pools, for they rarely survive the treatment there received, and the dhoby is perfectly careless of such sale-less articles. Tapes, too, and such like desirabilities, vanish most astonishingly; and single sewn garments return to the owner with such glaring disconnections as require great benevolence of character to witness.

The tailor is a most necessary part of the establishment of each house. His duties are to mend old linen, to cut out new dresses, and to make himself as generally useful in repairing dhoby-damages as he can. If the family consists of more than two persons his pay is from twelve to fifteen rupees per mensem, needles, thread, buttons, &c., being provided by the employer. Shirts are made by women, as also ladies' dresses, the charges on the latter varying according to the care and skill required. For shirts one shilling each is generally asked, and considering the great difference in money's worth here and in England, this compares most strikingly with the like payment at home for similar work.

Besides the trades already enumerated there are several to which no peculiar locality can be assigned, such as those of builders, painters, plasterers, &c. These are pursued with singular exclusiveness by a few, and an absurd limitation of the requirements from each forbids one man to encroach in the smallest way upon work that a neighbour considers as his profession; thus three or four persons are required to accomplish a small job that one man would execute at home in as short a space of time.

Having now taken a rapid survey of their chief haunts, it might be well to consider the manners and customs of the natives of this district, and thence to derive some general idea of their character in its connection with British rule in India.

NATIVE COCHIN.

CHAPTER IV.

THE MALABARS.

Causes producing the highlander's superiority to the inhabitant of plains—The native, his stature, weight, and strength—His wife, her physiognomy, proportions, and gait—The hair, little worn by men—Shaving—Woman's beauty—Phrenological students—Jewellery, ear, nose, finger, and toe rings—Curry and rice—Mode of eating—Selfish habits—Cleanliness, peculiar to higher classes—Want of musical ability.

THE aborigines of the Malabar coast are singularly inferior to those natives of Northern India whose fierce audacity has, from the earliest ages, deluged the interior with blood, brought famine and misery into the tropics, and paved the road for the stranger's entrance. And in this difference we may see those results of geographical position which, in a milder clime, have preserved the chivalrous character of the Swiss, Tyrolese, and Highlanders, amid the degeneracy and subjection of their lowland neighbours. Mountain ranges, as affording that certain protection which numbers are often unable to give, have invariably tended to make the tribes resident in their fastnesses bold and confident to such a degree as has, from the days of the Greeks to the Circassians, been productive of more disaster to Kings and Czars than the conquest of kingdoms. Climatic influences, necessitating a higher state of activity and a keener pursuit after the necessaries of life, have served also to make the high-country man more vigorous and self-reliant than the inhabitant of the plain, and though he does not possess that moderation of appetite when in possession of lowland luxuries, indispensable to the maintenance of his conquests, he has too much natural independence of character to relinquish all hope of regaining his freedom after defeat; and so, what with envy of the comforts of the lowlander, and vigorous actions to recover what he may have lost by the attempt to monopolise them, he has, at all times and in all countries, been a most important agent in promoting that civilisation which it might be imagined, at first sight, he would most greatly impede. We owe our wonderful supremacy here, most assuredly, to the mountain tribes; they for centuries quarrelled with one another, to the lasting disaster of all around, and eagerly accepted any terms for a white stranger's assistance, if they had reasons to hope that therefrom the subjection of the foe would more surely result. We have played no new game in India, much as we are blamed for our mode of acquisition; Alexander, Cæsar, and Hannibal, in ancient days, and (besides the conquerors in the middle ages) Napoleon the Great, and his remarkable nephew in our own times, have all learnt in the same school with ourselves, and been propelled by that invisible necessity of self-preservation to undertake wars which have changed the fate of the world again and again.

It would be unfair, in attempting to describe the Malabars, not to say beforehand that many a one is as tall, handsome, aud symmetrical as an artist could wish to sketch; but, taking a general view of the majority, it must be allowed that they are an inferior race, small, weak, and debased. The lowest and most numerous class of the men, working as coolies, sailors, and agriculturists, are, on an average, but five feet six inches high, and thin in proportion; with small heads, low frontal development, and large animal propensities, unmuscular in appearance, though anything but effeminate in reality; the hands thin but flexible; the legs narrow round the thighs, with protuberant knees, small calves, and wide-spreading feet, with the large toe stretched considerably away from the others. He weighs seven stone ten pounds, or about as much as the average of Englishwomen, or one-third less than most Englishmen. But this difference must not be necessarily associated with a want of power, for his diet is rice, a grain that absorbs a greater quantity of water in cooking, without imparting such a proportion of nourishing matter as animal food, but without, also, generating that heat and laziness which indulgence in the latter so especially does in the tropics. He is sometimes broad across the shoulders, but is seldom so plump as his wife in this respect, and he has a stooping habit after youth has passed which she never acquires till old age. He can carry stupendous weights on his head, and with most supreme callousness receive on it blows and contusions which might kill a white man.

He does not possess any great strength in raising weights, but as far as traction and propulsion is concerned, he is not by any means incapable. From being carried astride on his mother's hip in infancy, he is generally bow-legged, which gives him a steady but inelegant gait; he either swings his arms very fast with straightened fingers, or clasps them behind his back when walking, and takes steps very disproportionate to his height. His voice is harsh, guttural, and when raised in anger, discordant; but, with a few exceptions, the lower orders in Europe are distinguished by the same indifference to articulation.

The Malabar woman is mostly of a more robust build than the man. Her head is low and sometimes ill-shaped, but not generally so, the forehead broad if not high, boldly chiselled eyebrows, large lustrous jet-black eyes, *nez retroussé*, wide mouth, thick lips, excellent teeth, small and retreating chin. Broad, as before observed, across the shoulders, she is when young the same width round the hips, with by no means a waspish waist, and stands firmly on feet, which, as well as her hands, are small and well-shaped. She is about five feet one inch in height, and built in good proportion. Her weight is seldom over six stone three pounds, and often not more than five stone seven pounds, or about one-half that of an Englishman. Her walk is quick and bustling, right ahead, with but one object in view, and (excepting when carrying a baby) she holds herself upright and swings her arms most actively. Her voice is sometimes harmonious, but not generally so; as age draws on it becomes so shrill that its sound is quite painful, and though not particularly loquacious at other times, she acquires, if enraged, a volubility of utterance that might merit attention in St. Giles's. The colour of the Malabars differs greatly, and can be best imagined by taking a cup of coffee undiluted as the standard of low life, and pouring in drops of milk as higher rank is desired, until the white predominates in the liquid, which is the tint of the aristocratic classes.

The native has an abundance of coarse glossy black hair, like that of the true gipsy. The man, if a heathen, permits it to grow from one small circle on the crown of his head, prides himself much upon the length of the top-knot thus raised, and considers no insult so great as to have it pulled. The moustache and beard is seldom touched until the day before marriage, when they also are razed, and remain invisible until an addition to the family is expected, when they are again cultivated until the birth has taken place. The Hindoos are very particular in observing this custom, and also that of remaining unshaven for one year after a mother's death, which the progress of Christianity is gradually rendering obsolete. The hair or down on the breast and under the arms is taken off regularly, and naturally grows again with a rapidity and vigour that soon makes the native a veritable Esau. English razors are now pretty generally used, without soap, only a preparatory softening of the skin with water. The barber is very skilful, and the customer apparently "easy;" the operation goes on in the bazaar under a shed, or beneath a shady tree on the high road, and occupies a short space of time considering the bristly nature of the crop, the unevenness of the ground, and the paltry character of the instrument.

Plenteousness of hair in the woman is the chief standard of beauty among the natives, and all take great care of its growth and preservation. It grows rapidly until it reaches the hips, which appear to be its limit as much as the small of the back is that of the man's top-knot. It is washed about once a week, superfluously oiled, and most carefully cleaned with a large-toothed horn comb; but notwithstanding this, and the care of friends to remove the impurities, vermin propagate most painfully. On the high road a group may frequently be seen of a mother studying the phrenological peculiarities of an elder daughter, with an industry that can only be equalled by that daughter's observance of the development of a sister's head, who is herself engaged in perseveringly rubbing the little bald pate of the baby in her lap; sometimes the father lends a hand, and if he has a vow, he is also benefited by the assiduity of a young relative. Two friends meet, and squat down before each other; hardly a word is interchanged before two arms are raised benevolently to perform this office, with such dexterity as can only be acquired by early training. It is not an agreeable, though often a highly ridiculous sight, to observe the fixity of purpose portrayed in the countenances of these friendly investigators, as discovery stimulates research. The hair of the poorer orders seldom turns grey until they are thirty-eight or forty years of age; whereas that of the higher ranks is frequently white at thirty, in consequence, it is supposed, of the medicinal oils and unguents employed in beautifying its appearance in youth.

The dress of the Malabars differs most importantly in respect to caste and creed, but that of the working population may be very briefly described. The man twists round his loins a piece of cotton cloth about a yard long and two feet wide, by holding one corner against his waist, bringing the other tightly round, and tucking it in next to his skin. When actively employed he rolls the cloth up so that it shall not interfere with the free motion of his legs. He generally possesses also a piece of muslin, about the same size as his cloth, which serves as his turban in the day, and folded around his head and body as his protection at night, thus explaining the merciful injunction:

> 26. If thou at all take thy neighbour's raiment to pledge, thou shalt deliver it unto him by that the sun goeth down;
>
> 27. For that is his covering only: it is his raiment for his skin: wherein shall he sleep?—*Exodus* xxii.

The dress of the woman, if a heathen, is nearly the same as that of her husband, except that the muslin is flung loosely across the breast when she enters a town in which she may meet Europeans, for at other times she wears no breast-cloth whatever. The Christian woman has a tight-fitting jacket, made with three openings just large enough to admit her head and arms. The same dress is often worn without removal for a fortnight, and then perhaps, though not certainly, she bathes and puts on purer garments. On Sunday, however, she never fails to appear clean, though often with a robe underneath as foul as that above is snow-white. At church she wears a large muslin veil over her head and shoulders, and takes her place among other women similarly attired in the aisle opposite to that occupied by the men. The effect is exceedingly pleasing.

The Malabars have an insatiable taste for jewellery, and, no matter how humble in station and reduced in fortune, pander to it by the use of trinklets fabricated in the most precious and the most base of metals. Women and children of both sexes wear a tiny gold, silver, or tin box suspended by a piece of thread round the waist, and in this they store the small silver coinage of the country. Rings of gold, silver, copper, lead, and brass, chased with more or less care according to the metal, crowd the woman's fingers and toes; whilst bracelets and anklets fetter the movements of her arms and legs. The bracelets are frequently solid, but the anklets seldom consist of more than thin tubular rings, in which are placed some small balls which tinkle against the case with every step.* Necklaces of metal, glass, and wooden beads, with strings of flowers, are worn on feast days by all, but certain castes, such as the Dhobies, are never seen without a profusion of such ornaments. The most valuable necklaces, costing often fifteen hundred rupees, consist of a collection of foreign gold coins, tastefully set at regular intervals among bright beads, and pendants of the same metal. Roman coins of great antiquity and in excellent preservation may often be found side by side with

* The Jews of old appear to have adorned themselves in a fashion much in character with that generally considered to be peculiarly Indian. See Isaiah iii.

> 16. . . . the daughters of Zion are haughty, and walk with stretched forth necks and wanton eyes, walking and mincing as they go, and making a tinkling with their feet.
>
> 18. . . . the Lord will take away the bravery of their tinkling ornaments about their feet, and their cauls, and their round tires like the moon.
>
> 19. The chains, and the bracelets, and the mufflers,
>
> 20. The bonnets, and the ornaments of the legs, and the headbands, and the tablets, and the ear-rings,
>
> 21. The rings, and nose jewels,
>
> 22. The changeable suits of apparel, and the mantles, and the wimples, and the crisping pins.

A briefer or more expressive description of the Nautch or Dancing Girls of India could not be written.

Portuguese doubloons, Venetian sequins, Spanish pistoles, Russian imperials, Austrian ducats, and English sovereigns.

In the nostrils small gold rings and studs are inserted, the latter being bolted inside with a small peg. Sometimes the ring is two inches in diameter, and passes over the mouth in, one would imagine, a most inconvenient manner. Emeralds and rubies, or their representatives in glass, are strung upon the wire rather sparingly. The natives look upon the nose-rings as the greatest improvement to their appearance, but the association inevitably forced on a stranger's mind prevents his appreciation of the fashion.

The ear, however, suffers most in the sacrifice of comfort to show. A hole is pierced into it when the child is one year old, and the soft rib of a feather inserted; this after a little time is substituted by a peg of lead, which necessarily enlarges the aperture, is then taken out and replaced by a piece of palmyra leaf rolled into a spiral form, and possessing thence great power of expansion. After this has been in until the hole is too large to hold it longer, another of greater dimensions, or a circular piece of wood like the bung of a cask, is forced in, and often causes the flesh to tear asunder. The damage, however, is quickly repaired by wrapping part of the wing of a bat tightly round the ends, and anointing the whole with a salve of oil and herbs. With the stretcher inserted, the ears now stand out on either side of the head in a most painful manner, and one must feel convinced that woman is capable of far greater endurance in walking through Vanity Fair than man can boast of. After marriage, large plates of gold or horseshoe-shaped pendants are fastened around the string of flesh; but their use is only continued until the first child is born, and then the mother begins to divest herself of rings and chains, assumes more plain clothes, and rapidly degenerates into the miserable slit-eared hag of the Bazaar. The Mohammedan girl is not subjected to such tortures as must render her Hindoo and Christian playmates miserable, but yet does not reach womanhood without trouble, for the outer circumference of her ears is pierced with twenty to even thirty holes in succession, and into *each* of these a thin ring is fastened. There is not much to choose between either fashion, but perhaps the last is the least open to criticism, as the shape and natural position of the member is not much disturbed. It must not be imagined that the owner of so many golden, silver, or leaden charms divests herself before going to roost of her fifty or sixty ear-rings, for that would indeed be an objection to the custom. Doubtless habit soon familiarises one to such a taste, but at first uneasy must lie the head that wears such things.

Besides a profusion of the above ornaments, the girl on her marriage-day is literally covered with gold and silver chains, and crowned with a massive head-piece, beneath the weight of all which, and weakened by the numerous processions, she frequently faints. After the ceremonies are concluded the ornaments are carefully laid aside, and perhaps only employed during her lifetime in the decoration of a friend. After death the heir succeeds to these trinkets as to landed property, and preserves them with scrupulous care. He will give them as security for a debt, or as bail for a friend, but must be reduced to the utmost misery before he will sell them; for he feels even more pride in their possession than the English gentleman does in the shield, spurs, and banner of an illustrious ancestor "who came over with William the Conqueror."

Curry and rice form the staple food of all classes in India. The curry stuff consists of such articles as coriander, cummin, and ulva seeds, ginger, turmeric, and garlic, with tamarinds, onions, and small pieces of cocoanut, finely pounded together into a paste, in which vegetables, fish, or flesh are boiled. The articles curried are innumerable; they comprise almost all roots and fruits, with the leaves and soft heart of several trees. The high caste Hindoo will not touch fish or flesh, but the lower ranks make little demur to either, neither is the Christian or the Mohammedan particular on this point.

The rice is boiled in large earthen pots, with that wonderful success of making each individual grain stand on end of which even a Soyer would be innocent; and when ready is ladled on to a banana leaf and handed to the hungry spectator. He places it on his knees, and makes it up into a small hillock, and then, pressing his fist into the centre, moulds out a crater for the reception of the curry. This is now ready, and ladled out very carefully. The hungry one, with self-denying patience, employs his fingers assiduously in effecting a thorough association of both dishes, and then digs into the heap, opens his mouth very wide, and tosses the handful in without dropping a grain. He looks not to right or left; he has an undertaking to perform, and from the hungry rapidity of the hand's ascent it would seem that the time for its execution is very limited. At length the great heap has disappeared! whither, is almost as suggestive of astonishment as the conjuror's consumption of white wool. The stomach, besides its cast iron nature of digesting almost anything in the animal and vegetable kingdom, appears to have, in India, a power of expansion which might make even an Irishman stare with a recollection of his feats over a chaldron of potatoes. The natives take two meals a day of no perceptible difference in character, excepting that the article curried may be a root instead of a leaf. They do not drink much during their meals; if very thirsty, they may take a shellful of buttermilk or cunjee (the broth of rice), or a little cocoa-nut milk; but their food mainly consists of a grain that absorbs nearly three-fourths its weight of water, and any great indulgence in liquids is therefore quite unnecessary. The lower classes consume a large quantity of toddy when food is not plentiful. Between meals, small quantities of a slightly stimulating mixture are eaten. Upon a betel leaf, a portion of an areca-nut and a little lime, tobacco, and perhaps a few spices, are placed, tightly folded up into a ball, and thus thrown into the widely opened mouth. The whole is masticated with epicurean satisfaction, the lump in the cheek gradually lessens in size, and at length the ruminating action of the jaw ceases. The natives, both men and women, carry about a small treasure of these materials carefully swathed up in the corner of their cloth.

The mode of taking meals, general from the Rajah to the beggar, is peculiarly selfish and animal. The eyes glisten, the hand is zealous, the mouth obedient, but nothing of what constitutes the feature of civilisation, hospitality of manners, is yet to be seen in the polished Bramhan or the graceful Nair. Food is always eaten in a squatting position, and when consumed, the men either stretch themselves at full length and fall asleep on the spot, or sit lazily mooning in the doorway, whilst the wives repay themselves for their labour in waiting on their husbands, by consuming the residue of the meal. The knowledge of the barbaric ignorance of so many millions in the "Art of Dining" might have astonished the pleasant author of the Original.

The habits of the natives are not as a rule cleanly. A bath, though convenient from the neighbourhood of water, is seldom indulged in more than once in a week; meanwhile a handful of water tossed on the face is considered sufficient for the daily ablutions. The teeth are cleaned with the forefinger of the right hand, or with a piece of the branch in the spathe of the cocoa-nut tree beaten out at the end into bristly fibres; and charcoal is occasionally employed for powder, as otherwise they would be irremediably stained by the red juice of the betel leaf. The natives in this part have excellent teeth; and though toothache is experienced by some, the majority are free from this misery, as well as from bereavements by decay in youth. But if the lower classes are indifferent to cleanliness, the higher ranks are almost painfully attentive to it. Enjoined again and again in their sacred books to the observance of ceremonies during the bath and meal, they employ one-third of their waking existence in such devotional exercises, and fully another sixth in resting from them. The body is most carefully cleansed from all such foul impurities as the atmosphere in which Christians, Mahomedans, and others breathe, by rubbing oil into every pore of the skin, permitting it to absorb there for an hour, and then washing every trace of it off with water and small grains. The forehead, neck, breast, arms, and wrists, are now painted in a variety of fashions, according to the deity worshipped: in vertical or horizontal bars mostly. The paint consists of the ashes of sandal wood and cow-dung, mixed up with a little water into a paste, and thus crossed over the body with the fingers. The lower orders merely use the ashes of the latter. Besides its employment in designating the heathen's rank and faith, cow-dung, after mixture with sand, is universally made use of to daub the walls and floors of the huts and houses. The abundance of ammonia exhaled stops the inroad of insects, without, however, becoming in any way unpleasant to the residents. One caste, indeed, are enjoined to take every morning a solution of cow-dung in water for the promotion of inward purity.*

Music is singularly barbaric in this part of India. The faculty appears developed, indeed, but in that state of infancy which delights in sound independent of harmony; and progress seems very improbable without an entire reformation in the conservative temple pieces. It has been maintained that song and speech are coeval: it would seem so, from the sweet little ditty the baby composes and sings to itself before it can even speak; but association would, doubtless, to an European as to a Malabar, check the one power and foster the other. The natives have a keen delight for choruses,

* So large a demand for and consumption of such a material might reasonably excite surprise and disgust. But is it generally known that in our own country every printed cotton dress is steeped in a bath of this article previous to presentation before the engraved rollers, and that all the science of Europe has, as yet, failed to discover a material possessing superior properties for fixing the colours

and work really with greater zeal when permitted to exercise their lungs together. The boatmen on the Backwater sing until tired, with such a chorus that their advent can be looked for at a mile's distance. They take it by turns to conduct the concert, and invariably make allusions to the passengers in such a manner as to stretch the mouths of all the performers. When they arrive at or depart from a village, they unite in shouting several words denotive of the period of the voyage; and when rowing against a strong and dangerous current, they accompany every stroke with guttural interjections like those of the rascally Arabs who pull you up and down the Pyramids. The coolies also have their own songs with peculiar choruses, which stimulate their energies on the "pull-all-together" principle. But these songs are always deficient in harmony, though time is tolerably observed; and being generally the extemporary productions of hungry men, it may be conceived the subject is not very ennobling. In the temples the songs in honour of the Divinities are anything but agreeable in sound, and the accompaniments of the procession are only tolerable from a distance. Tom-tom, trumpet, cymbal, fife, and buzz,* unite in barbarous uproar, with apparently the same object in view as that of the Grecian musicians who considered strength of sound to be the standard of talent. The tom-tom is a small drum, suspended by a cord from the neck, and played with the whole weight of the hand, or with the fingers only. The trumpets differ very much in shape and size, though but little in the hysterical screams they produce.

* This is not the actual name of the instrument, but for want of a more expressive denomination it is hoped the coinage will be pardoned.

The flute is capable of emitting sounds as sweet as those of the flageolet, but it is generally played in too high a key. The buzz is a portion of a large reed, with a mouthpiece and an internal economy which only permits a sound to escape like that of an enormous bee. The Romans appear to have had an instrument much like this, but coupled with another, so that the two pipes might be blown together and played with the left and right hand, and thence called respectively the *tibia sinistra* and the *tibia dextra;* the former, we read, giving a deep serious bass, whilst the latter had a sharp and lively sound. The temple pieces of music vary little in character: the time is highly *vigoroso*, and the cadence very rapid; and associated with banners, flowers, and gay crowds, they are doubtless calculated to excite the native; but they savour too much of the bagpipes, hurdy-gurdy, and penny trumpet to please a stranger.

Some attempts have lately been made to train the Christian girls to sing in church, and with a success creditable alike to the perseverance of the instructors and the good-will of the students; but the difficulties have been so great to get the voices unitedly into tune, and to keep them so, even with the assistance of an organ, that we must really believe there is a natural deficiency in the native's appreciation of sound and calculation of time.

NATIVE COCHIN.

CHAPTER V.

THE MALABARS.

The standard whereby to judge a people—Maternal regard—Neglect—Mortality among infants — Education — Marriage — Conjugal, paternal, and filial affection—Sad diseases—Hereditary complaints—Death—Funeral ceremonies—Feasts and anniversaries—Will-making—Inheritance— Heir-looms—Law of mortgage—Ideas formed by intercourse with natives—Their character considered with reference to British rule.

In examining the characteristics of a peculiar race, and endeavouring thence to deduce some broad rules by which a judgment may be formed of its influence upon the world at large, no better criterion can be taken than that afforded by its observance of relative duties. Indeed, the race, to be viewed as a whole, must be considered as an individual, and the same observations made on its character as we are accustomed to employ in judging of a man's disposition, which, however noble and apparently unselfish towards his fellows, is certain to be estimated in the end by his conduct towards his family.

The Malabar woman naturally possesses that amount of tenderness for her offspring which is common to the brute creation. She endures much fatigue in rearing it, and seems to take a pride in its healthy, well-fed condition. Occasionally she is, however, sadly deaf to the pitiful cries of her child after she has placed it on a mat in some dark corner of the hut, and the poor little thing, unable to turn from side to side, at length frets itself to sleep, and early learns habits of self-dependence; and as the constitution of many is too feeble to endure this neglect, the mortality among infants is very great. This, perhaps, should not be entirely charged upon the mother, for by the time the child is a year old she generally has another call on her attention, and yet must work ten hours a day to assist her husband in their support. Maturity is attained in this hot land at an age that renders it impossible for the young wife to acquaint herself with maternal duties before marriage, and afterwards she has but little leisure for their study. The child generally grows up without any great expenditure of affection on the part of either parent, and passes the first two years of its existence straddling the mother's hips, only in a very slight degree restricting her movements or engaging her attention. If no other child has been born meanwhile, it is frequently not weaned until it is three years old, and from that age until five it runs about without any clothing, but always with a chuckrum box tied with a thin cord round its fat little stomach. It has probably picked up several words from parents and playmates, and is now sent to a native school, and by small degrees learns to decipher letters on the ollahs, and to exereise a little mental calculation; but, as a rule among the natives, the education is entirely oral and of a singularly illiberal character. The parents sometimes take the trouble to instil into the child such abstract ideas of religion as they possess, and in the neighbourhood of missionaries, excellent schools are established to remedy any deficiency; but elsewhere the knowledge communicated is painfully minute and grossly erroneous.

Marriage, or rather betrothal, takes place when the ages of the man and woman are respectively nineteen and twelve. Among Christians, the bride remains with her father two or three years after the ceremony, and is then, with her dowry, conducted to her husband's house. After fifteen the Hindoo girl has little chance of being married at all; she is first thought of, and then treated as an inferior being, is compelled to do the hardest work in the house, and consequently is soon found among the very dregs of the population. This is exceedingly sad, and parents feel such a reflection of the disgrace as prompts their best endeavours for the early settlement of each daughter, and so spinsters are generally scarce. There is no sympathy for misfortune, but a hard-hearted contempt of the individual for what is declared to be the penalty of her own misconduct, and thus despised, and even ill-treated, it is not surprising if the unmarried girl sinks into infamy. Parents and friends appeal to this declension as a proof of their foresight, and in future most uncharitably predict the same end for some other girl, and by thus destroying her self-respect, almost invariably induce the results they pretend to deplore. But even where the relations are less cruel the unmarried woman among heathen and insufficiently educated Christians leads an hopeless life as the servant of servants. The married woman on the contrary receives the respect of her neighbours, and for the first two or three years seems comparatively comfortable; but at eighteen her face begins to assume a melancholy care-worn appearance, and at twenty she is in her wane. In public there is never any display of conjugal sympathy, and in private it is to be feared but little is practised; the kiss of affection is not known, and even the shaking of hands has only very recently been imitated from the Europeans. Very possibly the natives have sentiments less demonstrative than ours, and small actions may be peculiarly construed, yet it is not easy to account for the absence of affectionate looks, which even a dog can express for a loved master. Quarrelling between husband and wife is frequent, and relish for the "last word" often obtains for the latter a dreadful beating; but if the man is small and the lady strong the tables are frequently turned. After a time the wife gets accustomed to abuse and complaints, and submits with exemplary patience. A little warmth of feeling is apparent when the first child arrives, and the young father hugs the little thing very kindly, but this sympathy wears away very soon, and its brothers and sisters are viewed with comparative indifference.

A son is always regarded with much more favour than a daughter: for he is firstly of much importance in contributing to the support of the family; he is an assistance during the parents' life, and at their death he performs the obsequies in their honour, and thereby propitiates the gods, which, it is held, no stranger can effectually do. The daughter, on the other hand, can earn but little for the general welfare, and on her marriage is expected to have some dowry, and her connection with her kith and kin is then permanently severed;

whilst unmarried she continues to live with her parents, until ill-treatment brings about either her ruin or early death. There is unhappily a want of filial affection for the mother when she gets old and enfeebled, her presence in a son's house is merely tolerated, and her demise looked upon as a relief. Aged fathers do not obtain much more consideration, and the more children they have brought up the less are they esteemed, which may be attributable to the indifference with which parents here regard the successors of the firstborn.* Christianity however is tending to eradicate the selfishness of the native's character, and implant charitable feelings instead, and the exercise of benevolence is soon proved by an astonishing change in the lines of his mouth, and more especially in the expression of his eyes.

Unwholesome and scanty diet, damp dwellings and bad drainage, parental neglect and dissipation, have made the Malabars heirs to many of those lingering and shocking diseases that have baffled the treatment of modern science. In British and Native Cochin the malady brought most prominently under one's notice is Elephantiasis; and though in parts of Africa, the West Indies (Barbadoes especially), and in the Lincolnshire fens, this dire complaint is met with, it appears to be so extraordinarily severe in this district that in Ceylon and India generally it is known as the "Cochin leg." It appears in childhood, in early youth, and occasionally late in life; so little assistance is afforded to a solution of the question of its

* It must be remarked here that allusion is being made especially to the manners of the *lower* orders, for in the more educated classes we find the same tender, deferential feelings (or at least expressions) towards parents as distinguish the intercourse of relations in more civilised lands.

being hereditary. Certain it is, that natives often marry when its first symptoms are discernible, and no fear exists of contagion or procreation; but the fact of children being attacked by it strongly supports the objection of Europeans to such unions. The skin of the foot thickens, and some gelatinous matter collects beneath and gradually hardens; the calves and thighs are in turn affected, and at length the leg is so swollen that the foot is almost concealed. The flesh becomes very impassive, and does not pit on pressure, whilst the skin appears dark, rough, and scaly. In some patients but one leg is diseased, in others both; the rest of the body is meagre in the extreme, the circumference of the waist being often but little larger than that of the leg around the thigh or over the foot. It is some relief to the distress a spectator must experience on viewing this awful disease, to learn that it is only accompanied by pain about once a month, or at longer intervals, when the swelling increases; and that, unlike the gout, it never ascends higher than the thighs, and does not as a rule tend to shorten life. The sinews, muscles, and bones remain in a comparatively healthy condition; and, excepting the periodical fevers and difficulty in locomotion, the patient is providentially spared much misery by the insensitiveness of the member. Cases are on record of the swellings decreasing by entire change of air and the use of pure water, and of the patient remaining free from the disease during his absence from Cochin, and of being attacked again immediately on his return. A few faint hopes are entertained that eventually some light will be thrown on the subject by the persevering investigation of our surgeons.

In the interior, away from large towns, Leprosy is met with under the most painful circumstances. First appearing in youth as a few eruptions dispersed in groups on the arm below the elbow, and on the leg below the knee, it gradually widens its influence, and the smaller spots are merged into great patches, of which the centre is delicately white, and the circumference slightly red. The patients are now obliged to leave society, and generally form a small community among themselves, or resort to the hospitals which Government has established in various parts of the country for their protection. The fingers and toes often fall off, and the stumps of hands and feet only are left; and such is the affliction of a man who is cut off from communion with his kind, incapable of earning a livelihood, and who was dependent entirely upon his hands for subsistence. Imagination can hardly conceive a greater curse on humanity; for though many diseases are yet more hideous to behold, they are frequently the result of the sufferer's own misconduct, whereas the leper may have led a most exemplary life in every way. Many commentators are of opinion that the leprosy mentioned in the Bible may be understood as elephantiasis, but the allusions to the "leper as white as snow standing afar off" do not seem to permit of such a construction, which would certainly lessen the value of the miracles; we can imagine a huge swelling of flesh rapidly subsiding, and that the restoration of the afflicted to long-lost vigour would cause him much joy; but what satisfaction could be so intensified as that of a leper—an outcast—suddenly returning to health and society, and what could excite the awe of bystanders so much as witnessing so benevolent, so instantaneous, so marvellous a cure?

The first appearance of Small-pox in India is involved in much uncertainty. Many hold that it was coeval (as in America) with the arrival of the Europeans; but there certainly has from earlier periods been a disease here that corresponds in most particulars to the plague of Athens in the time of Pericles, which classics, reasonably enough, conjecture was small-pox. The natives hold it in great fear, and until the dawn of this century were of course at its mercy. Their treatment is interesting. After three days' preliminary fever, a cooling decoction of roots, leaves, and herbs is administered, and another when the disease is at its height; the pustules are pricked with a thorn, and the wounds sprinkled with a powder manufactured from thoroughly dried goat's-dung, turmeric, and some aromatic leaves. The juice of small onions is squeezed into the eyes to prevent ophthalmia, and during the day a little is taken with sugar internally. The malady is thus treated during a period varying from twelve to twenty days; the patient then bathes three times, and is pronounced convalescent. The native princes have for many years kept several itinerating vaccinators in their pay; and after a long contest with superstitious objections, the benefits of Dr. Jenner's wonderful discovery have at length been communicated to all castes and creeds without exception. The Civil Surgeon of Cochin has a number of small out-stations, in each of which a native vaccinator is placed under his immediate directions, so no excuse is permitted to the inhabitant of the most remote district for not protecting himself betimes. A wise order from Government requires the vaccination of *all* persons on their entrance into the jail of British Cochin; and it is to be hoped that the Rajah will soon enforce it upon all *his* subjects.

The unhealthy nature of so extensively irrigated a country as that around Cochin is eminently successful in propagating itches, fever, diarrhœa, dysentery, cholera, and rheumatism. For itches, which are a very plague to the lower classes, a decoction of sarsaparilla and herbs is taken, and the sores carefully rubbed with old cocoa-nut oil and sulphur. For fever herb pills are administered, with external applications to the head and eyes. For rheumatism (a very common complaint) different kinds of oils are used, and heating decoctions of medicinal roots taken periodically. For cholera the native doctors administer some very small pills containing mercury and other powerful substances. The patient is not allowed any nourishment for four and twenty hours, and is only permitted to slake his thirst with warm water in which some herbs have been boiled; garlic, &c., being rubbed over the limbs to relieve cramp. The mortality from spasmodic cholera is sometimes frightful. In the jail at Calicut lately, more than one hundred persons died out of four hundred during five days; and, to prove that the habits of life have *some* influence on the disease, it is stated that the very worst characters were attacked. In the monsoon months, when food is scanty, active employment difficult to obtain, and temperature rapidly changeable, cholera becomes epidemic; whole families are often taken off in a few hours, and many poor wretches endeavour to drown all fear in sensual indulgence, and in this condition are swept away.

There are many diseases arising from bad water, and more especially from improper living, which the native doctors do not seem to comprehend at all; and in some neighbouring villages the disfigurements from the latter cause strike the spectator with horror. And what is still more shocking to see, the children about are but too often infected with the same inextricable disorders, and yet play with others in the most unrestrained manner. Hereditary complaints die out of a family much less slowly in India than in England; for, on account of caste feeling, there is here but little opportunity for a man of the lower orders to rise to a position superior to that in which he was born, and consequently the same habits of life, and generally the same class of associates, are retained from generation to generation; whereas in England it is very uncommon to meet three successions of a family in precisely the same condition of life: industry and talent have a clear stage for exercise, and new hopes, new thoughts, new habits are formed, which have a wonderful effect in destroying the idiosyncrasy at least of complaint, and then its treatment becomes comparatively easy.

The natives have a strong objection to being bled with a lancet, though the application of leeches is endured with considerable composure. Bruises and sprains are carefully fomented with herbs and rubbed with oil, but surgical operations are never attempted. Sometimes a toddy-drawer falls from the cocoa-nut tree, a height of sixty to seventy feet, and is picked up almost lifeless; but the neighbours carry the poor fellow at once to the nearest pool, dip him again and again, occasionally stretch his limbs, and then take him to his house and rub cocoa-nut oil over his joints until he shows good signs of recovery. This is a very fair specimen of the simple expedients of the natives: it is a rough kind of treatment truly, but generally eminently successful when no bones are broken.

The approaching death of a friend is regarded by the natives with singular composure, and (if the expression of the face may be considered) want of sympathy. Though he may be speechless and evidently failing fast, jokes are frequently made, and conversation carried on as on ordinary occasions. The wife kneels beside the head of the sufferer, applying such lotions as have been prescribed, and acts in a kind, but not in what can be called an affectionate, manner. The Hindoos remove the dying man out of the house, as were he to expire there it would be defiled, and place him upon a mat in the open air; for by their faith the spirit is encumbered with the weight of the article on which it departed from the body, and a couch would, consequently, be an objection in its upward flight. Immediately after death the corpse is washed, and swathed in clean cloth or muslin, which is fastened by small ribbons torn out of the material. The relations and neighbours now assemble, and, sitting around the body, watch; quiet is maintained, and a strict fast observed until all the preparations have been made for the burial, which generally takes place within six hours after death. The body is lifted up from the middle of the room or yard, and carried out upon a bier into the road, where the hired mourners are collected. A wail is unitedly set up, and answered by musical instruments, which emit their very wildest notes on these melancholy occasions. Bramhans are always burnt, but the other castes are generally buried, though if the deceased had expressed no preference the relations endeavour to perform the more honorable and expensive rites. The pile is three feet high, and about the length and breadth of a camp bed; for an affluent person sandal-wood faggots are employed, but for others pieces of mango, jack, and such jungle trees are sufficient; one small chip of costly wood is sometimes added. The friends stand around until the whole is consumed; and then the chief mourner, the son, brother, or nephew, collects the ashes into a basket made of a cocoa-nut leaf, or into a new earthen pot, and throws them into the sea or river on the banks of which these ceremonies are usually held. The Mussulmans bury their dead with most melancholy lamentations. On returning from the grave, or pile, a feast is given by the chief mourner to all who have assisted in the day's duties, and in the case of very rich people, the anniversary is observed for years with the same respect to the deceased. Many shun all gaiety for one year after the death, but this is only in honour of the nearest relations. Immense sums are often spent on the funeral and the subsequent feasts, for the native seems to reckon the degree of a man's sorrow according to the amount of inheritance he expends in memory of his friend. During the new moon in the month of June, the Hindoos have a solemn feast, at which it is believed the shades of their departed relations assemble; mats are spread on the ground, and banana leaves well piled with food placed upon them; and though the morning light shows that the material part of the nourishment is undiminished, it is imagined that the spirits have thoroughly appreciated it in a more refined manner.

It is not usual for a native to make his will until he apprehends the near approach of death, and as tropical sicknesses are very short, and the man is seldom so resigned as to relinquish all hope of recovery, the majority of people die intestate. In that event the nearest relations take charge of the property, collect and realise the estate, and divide it among the heirs. In Cochin territory the singular law of *murroo-muka-tayum*, or inheritance by sister's son, prevails among all the Hindoos except the Bramhans, whose marriage it is held is legal, whereas that of the lower castes is not, and therefore the children arising from such unions are illegitimate. Even the Rajah has to submit to this very unnatural law, and the succession to tho throne is always indirect. Popular prejudice is happily setting against it, and parents contrive to evade its regulations by making provision for children during their own lifetime, and obtaining the sanction of the Government to the gifts. In other parts of Malabar the Nairs are the only caste subject to it, and other Hindoos beside Mohammedans, Christians, &c., enjoy the privilege of *muka-tayum*, or succession of sons.

The property is generally collected ten days after the funeral, and then divided in conformity with the will, if any is found; but otherwise the sons inherit an equal share, and the widow has the care of everything, and a right to reside with the youngest child in the house in which her husband died. It is usual for a man to transfer property to his childless wife during his lifetime, and obtain a record of the gift on stamped paper, so that she shall not be left penniless in event of his death; but if he dies without making such provision, she has to return at once to her parents or any friends who may feel disposed to support her. As entail is unknown in the country, every man has a right to dispose of his property without any reference to his children, and in punishment of foolish sons this plan is sometimes resorted to, so as to make them residuary legatees of mere trifles; but it is exceedingly rare to find such disunion in families. The father is obliged to bequeath something tangible to every son, and so perhaps he cuts one off with half a rupee, the equivalent of a shilling. Jewellery and other heir-looms are the general property of the sons, but the eldest most frequently buys the shares of the others in order to prevent their distribution. Houses, also, and plantations, may be inherited in the same way, and sometimes the brothers live altogether, and carry on their father's business without dividing the estate; but after their marriage there are sure to be some conjugal troubles from the residence together of two or three families, and one of the brothers usually pays the others an equivalent for their portions, with which they depart and form separate establishments. One son cannot effect a sale of any part of the inheritance without the consent (on stamped paper) of his brothers; and the mother cannot dispose of any portion of the estate without the approval and signature of the children or their paternal uncles. Daughters cannot inherit by will, so the father transfers something over to them during his lifetime in the same manner as he would provide for a childless wife; but as they generally receive a dowry on their marriage it is not usual to make any further gifts to them. Friends are sometimes remembered in the will much to the prejudice of the children; this is, however, not frequent, as the native objects to his property losing its unity, and has a strong desire to perpetuate his individuality in connection with it.

It is customary in these parts to raise money by mortgage of lands and houses in time of need, and very precise laws are enforced for the benefit of all parties concerned. The deed must be drawn up on stamped paper, in which it is stated that the repayment of the loan is to be made within a certain period, that the mortgagee is to receive interest at a fixed rate per mensem, and (or) the rent of the houses and the produce of the land; and *sometimes* that the mortgage is to be returned at any time before it falls due on the payment of principal, interest, and charges. In the event of the mortgagor failing to make good his promise, a suit is made to the Court, and its decree obtained, which allows a month for the defendant to appeal to higher quarters, and after the expiration of that period the plaintiff enforces the decree, and the Court orders the sale of the property, the payment of all the mortgagee's claims, aud the presentation of any surplus of such sale to the mortgagor. Sometimes the defendant will not quit the ground, and then the purchaser has to institute a suit against him to effect his ejectment. In the case of a transfer of the property to the mortgagee, the mortgagor possesses for twelve years the right or equity of redemption, and can bequeath this right to his heirs, who, in a land where property so rapidly increases in value, often avail themselves of the benefit of so excellent a law.

An examination of the character of the Malabars is not calculated to induce satisfaction with human nature in a comparatively uncivilised condition. Poets of days when it was perilous to seek for information by travelling, have written most delightfully about

> "the poor Indian, whose untutored mind
> Sees God in clouds, or hears him in the wind;"

and even in the exquisite idyls of modern laureates a heathen is frequently described as the *beau-ideal* of humanity. But intercourse with the natives, costly experience of placing confidence in them, and observation of their conduct one towards another, entirely dissipate all preconceived notions of their honesty and benevolence. Christianity is doing much to ameliorate their character, and its influences must continue to spread, but they are necessarily slow in operation, and much has yet to be done to root out the deplorable selfishness and deceit bred by heathenism, and to supply instead a sense of moral obligation.

The aborigines of these parts, as has been already said, are not to be compared with the people in North India. They are doubtless deficient of most of their good qualities, but want the courage to view the prospect of defeat with resolution, and thus have from the earliest times submitted to the extortionate oppression of their Zamorins and Rajahs. These rulers, until very recently, have acted upon the most avaricious, shortsighted, and inhuman principles; tithes and taxes were first charged upon all landholders, produce itself was then seized, and finally seed was given for cultivation, and returns of crops looked for and enforced under all circumstances, until at length the patience of their subjects was exhausted, and the most frightful deeds perpetrated. The highest as well as the lowest officials had (and too frequently continue to have) their price; judgment was certain to be awarded in favour of the largest bribe; and the poor man found no court of appeal which would justly weigh and decide upon his case. So the natives became callous and inoffensive simply from oppression: they saw no remedy for the time to come, and consequently made the best of their present condition; and seeing the inordinate passions of their superiors, they soon learned to imitate their grovelling dishonest modes of obtaining wealth. It can be conceived that such treatment as they laboured under was most unfavourable to the development of proper principles; indeed it was so: stingy, miserly habits are almost universal; the love of money for its power, the necessity of hoarding it to prevent exaction; dishonest practices; a want of truth and conscientiousness; the absence of benevolence and charity; unhappiness caused by want of confidence in any man, and the constant indulgence of envious, avaricious, revengeful feelings; such have been the unsightly fruit, partly of regal tyranny, but more especially of the destruction of conscience by heathenism.

The above causes very naturally stimulated the worst passions of man. A relation's well-being, a neighbour's reputation, becomes a matter of envy to even a rich and honoured man; towards the former injustice is often shown in the settlement of an inheritance, and against the latter slanderous accusations are made. The native courts afford too much facility for one man to injure another by expensive law suits; and the system of appealing against a judgment on a frivolous matter from place to place, enables the rich man to distress a poorer one without any appearance of bad feeling. Cases have been known where a man has accused a neighbour of murder when the body of a suicide had been found, and until British influence overspread the country it sometimes ran hard against the defendant. In Ceylon, some fifty years ago, a most singular instance of such a malicious spirit occurred. A man, who had for some reason imbibed a strong feeling of enmity against a neighbour, endeavoured by imaginary charges to ruin his character and estate, but found English judges would not tolerate such proceedings, nor accept golden spectacles to view them; so as a last resource he went down to the sea beach, and deliberately committed suicide, under the impression that even British justice would be compelled to deem the neighbour (who was known to possess bad feelings towards him) guilty of his murder. But happily an *alibi* was established immediately the suspicion was aroused, and so the poor deluded Cingalese made a very useless sacrifice of himself.

Though for other objects most parsimonious, the native will, to gratify a little wicked feeling, expend large sums for the injury of another, and yet be so tricky in his actions that his malice may for long be unknown. He will serve and benefit an enemy for years, for the sake of ultimate revenge by obtaining his confidence, and

> "He can smile, and murder while he smiles,
> And cry content to that which grieves his heart,
> And wet his cheeks with artificial tears,
> And frame his face to all occasions."

The Malabars have very little friendliness or cheerfulness in their composition; not that they are exactly of a bilious temperament, for their appreciation of good fortune is vigorous; but excepting as regards their own comfort and gratification, they seldom view the happiness of another with any but malicious feelings. Sensitive to a degree of injustice towards themselves, and loudly indignant at a neighbour's dishonesty, they will not shrink from any small deceit that may injure another against whom they have a spite.

The women are, as a rule, obedient and subject to their husbands, never forgetful of their marriage vows, nor wasteful in the expenditure of property. On the other hand, the men are but too often immoral, lax in the performance of conjugal and parental duties, and cruel in their behaviour towards their wives. The woman is considered in every way inferior to the man; she is useful to him, cooks his food, rears *his* children, and watches his property; but being almost always uneducated, he views her with condescending contempt, and of course never imagines or attempts to promote what is called domestic happiness.

In recent years assault, highway robbery, and murder were most common in all parts. Travelling either on the Backwater or on land was most unsafe, and deeds were perpetrated every night under the most shocking circumstances. One rich miscreant near Cochin had in his employ an immense-limbed agile slave, whom he furnished with every assistance for murdering the passengers along the stream. The slave's success was great, and the profit arising from the devilry considerable, when one night he returned and presented his master with the bangles, jewels and chains that had that very day been placed upon a daughter on her marriage. With hopeless agony the father enquired what had been done to the wearer, and learnt to his horror that both she and her young husband had been murdered and sunk in the deep water. This was one of the last of such frightful deeds. In 1802 Mr. Drummond, the Collector and Commissioner of Malabar, adopted most severe measures to put down these barbarities; and by bold, but absolutely necessary threats, at length succeeded in intimidating the fiends incarnate who infested this land. Since that date travelling has become safe; and thanks to the unflinching justice and keen investigation of the British Government, security of life, limb and property is now assured to every man in even native territory.

Murder is not frequent among native Christians, nor is it often committed by any class but the Moplahs. Infanticide is most uncommon, which of course is attributable to the good behaviour of the women in married life. Brutal bullying, resulting sometimes in the victim's death, is often brought under one's notice, and more than anything induces intense disgust with the native character. If one or two men have a grudge against another they club together, seek out others who have also some grievance, and at length meet the object of their hatred alone. They surround, mob, kick, and punish him with the foulest blows, not standing up one by one and allowing the poor wretch to have a chance of defending himself, but altogether; and frightened of the consequences no man will strike a mortal blow, but each gratifies his malice by kicking and cuffing, and so beaten, the victim often dies under their hands. Then manslaughter can only be charged against them; and in a herd of such cowards it is difficult to discriminate which is the most arrant rascal, and of course useless to believe the testimony of a Queen's evidence, so they all get off with a punishment trifling as compared to the offence. In convictions of murder in Native Cochin, the sentence cannot be carried out without the confirmation of the Governor of Madras, and such approval is also required in our own territory. The last murder in British Cochin was in 1848, when a man killed a woman on the sea beach; circumstantial evidence pointed to him, and an examination in the Cutcherry confirmed the suspicion; he was sent on for trial by the Civil and Sessions Judge at Calicut, found guilty, and sentenced to be brought back here, hanged on the spot where he had committed the crime, and buried beneath the gallows. Cases have occurred in the twelve years since tantamount to, but not legally speaking, murder; but they have been generally more attributable to some immorality or extortion on the part of the deceased than to the indulgence of such intensely cruel passions as stimulated crime years ago.

It might very naturally be imagined that to possess territory adjoining that inhabited by such a class of people would ensure constant anxiety for its maintenance; and had it not been for the depressing effect of misgovernment, extortion, and barbarity, there can be no doubt that the million and a quarter Malabars would have been our most fierce enemies, and most unwilling subjects. Happily, however, for the peace of South India we have met with but trifling opposition in this province, and have derived, and must continue to derive, security from the disunion naturally existing between its many strange races. It is ruled nominally by Rajahs with much of the pomp and glitter, the sycophantic accompaniments of olden times, and so far as the distribution of empty honours, and the confirmation of trifling appointments is concerned, there is little for them to desire; but we have taken very good care to release them from such power as might be brought to bear disagreeably upon us; and with philanthropic representations of that hacknied war-cry of modern times, *the good of the people*, and tender consideration for the security of their petty sovereigns, we have entered into treaties by which very handsome tributes are annually paid her Britannic Majesty, and all virtual authority vested in her representatives. Failure in performing the former part of these treaties will be followed instantaneously by remonstrance, and perhaps ultimately by the annexation of their dominions; and discontent with our use of the latter must be masticated with the recollections of former might. To some jealous rivals in India the system by which we control native kingdoms appears highly extortionate, if not cruel; but we must feel convinced that our supremacy, and connected with it the peace of two hundred millions of fellow-beings, is dependent upon our setting our face boldly against all native craft and oppression; and by making the Rajahs answerable to us for their actions, as well as subject to our good-will for the maintenance of their thrones, we have compelled them to see at least the great danger of misruling, and thus have promoted the permanent security and happiness of all. In Malabar for the last half century the Moplahs have been the only tribe who have shown any dissatisfaction with our influence; and even they—a malignant and bigoted sect of Moslems, who imagine that the hinges of the gates of heaven can be greased with the blood of a heretic—even they are becoming aware of the value of honest rule, and as traders or smugglers are as intent upon hoarding money as they formerly were upon bloodshed and cruelty. Occasionally a few desperate villains have perpetrated the most horrid crimes, been discovered, and hunted from place to place until at length they took their stand in a house; and after a display of bravery worthy of a better cause have fallen one after another deriding the idea of surrender. Such a gang murdered Mr. Conolly, the Collector of Malabar, in 1855; and for small grievances have before and since that year proved that they cannot be trusted yet; but commerce is wonderfully improving their character, and within a few years may destroy the excellence in rascality that they now enjoy in the province. When up in arms they are most unpleasant antagonists; they throw away the scabbard truly, and fight to the death with such a fierce recklessness that our Hindoo sepoys have been often foiled in an attack, and have met with such dreadful punishment that it was a difficult matter to lead them on again: so it has been thought advisable to station European troops in the district, and since that has been done tranquillity has been generally maintained. There can be no doubt that had the Moplahs and some other tribes felt our supremacy irksome, there would have been little hesitation in taking advantage of the mutiny of our Bengal army in 1857, more especially as they must have known the embarrassment of our affairs; but, happily, they remained perfectly quiet, and afforded us the best promise of their future good behaviour. Added to this there is cause for satisfaction in the gradual disbandment of our native troops, and their substitution by Europeans, and every security seems to be afforded of Malabar continuing to enjoy the blessings of peace.

NATIVE COCHIN.

CHAPTER VI.

THE RAJAH.

His Kingdom as compared to that of his ancestors—His supposed descent—General principles of government—The slaves, their origin and debased condition—Effects of constant wars—Treaties with E. I. Co.—Relations existing with British Government—The present Rajah's reign, character, habits, &c.—The Royal Family—Succession to the throne—Revenue—The Dewan, his duties—Standing army—Administration of justice—Courts of law—The future of Cochin.

THE geographical position of the kingdom of Cochin, like that of the many small provinces which, merged together, have assisted to form our colossal Indian empire, has been unfavorable to the civilisation of its inhabitants by the ameliorating influences of prolonged peace. Its frontier, always irregular and detached, pursued the track of the Rajah's victorious army, or the limits of the incursion of a neighbour, and not any line of demarcation which nature had erected to show its safest bounds; and thus it once included a noble extent of soil, but subsequently relaxed into the small dimensions of which a glancc at the map will show the significant weakness. With the exception of Switzerland, it would be difficult to enumerate the kingdoms in Europe which, surrounded by other Powers, have not forfeited their independence; and Switzerland is so cup-like in its formation, that nature seems to have resolved that no invading foot shall ever press the sward of its delightful soil. Cochin may not, with truth, be exactly described as in the interior, for it does possess a coast line, but of so short and unimportant a nature that the proximity of the ocean is a greater cause for fear than satisfaction. The possession of the entrance into the great system of rivers which permeate the surrounding states should have been considered invaluable; but it has been seen how easily it was given up to the Portuguese, and it may therefore be imagined that its importance was not duly estimated in former times. Land, not sea, warfare was doubtless the most frequent, and in it the Rajah experienced so many obstructions by the constant presence of rivers, and so few advantages by the possession of disconnected highlands, that not only must his conquests have been achieved with great difficulty, but the maintenance of the original boundaries of his territory must have at all times been a most anxious task.

In countries like this, where the trees produce food for both man and horse, there seem to be fewer objections to war and stimulants to peace than in our own clime; for war is able to support war in the most important sense, and the soil is so generous that seed-time and harvest might have been included in the operations of a besieging army of former days. The jungles not only produced fruit and leaves, but wood for bows, poison for arrows, and most things necessary to an invading army; and the weather being regular, exposure to it unimportant, none of those diseases were induced which fell more soldiers than showers of grape-shot. But, whilst nature seems to have made war easy in India, a just provision is found to render aggression in the end unfortunate; for these facilities which assist an army's march cannot be much impaired, and the miserable inhabitants returning to their haunts, find their houses sacked and their lands impoverished; but the trees and fields soon again give abundant returns, and energy is thus revived to rebel against and overthrow the oppressors. Where man fights with rude weapons that can be reproduced without delay, only requiring vegetables of a land like this for his support, and a square yard of linen to clothe him, he is inclined to become finely sensitive of his own rights, and wonderfully forgetful of his neighbour's; he is not absolutely compelled to sit down and count the cost before assuming the aggressive, but rather is tempted to war by its apparent facility. Great conquests might be made, like those of the able monarchs of Seringapatam, but to retain the advantages long enough to transmit them to a son, required the sleepless head, the determined will, the decisive foresight of Hyder Ali. For these reasons the soil of India has imbibed more human blood than perhaps any land of similar size elsewhere; and under such a consideration, with an idea of what used to be the condition of the country as compared with what it now is, we may look upon the extended manufacture of costly and scientific munitions of war as a most valuable assistance towards promoting long-lived peace.

The ancient history of Cochin is involved in hazy obscurity up to the days of Ceram Perumal, who flourished in the eighth or ninth century. A few detached fables have been learned from existing *ollahs*, but none of sufficient value to show the system of government, or the condition of the country before his time. The art of engraving upon the palmyra leaf being confined, even in the present day, to a comparatively small proportion of the inhabitants, it may be presumed that in olden times, when war and tumult were the chief objects of care, the number of scribes must have been most insignificant, and their intellectual capacity of a very low grade. This carelessness of the people to record their history may betoken an absence of that self-confidence and satisfaction, as well as of that ingenious ability which made the Mexican expert in manufacturing historical pictures with the varied plumage of the lovely birds of his country, and suggested symbols by which the Egyptian and Peruvian have instructed nations then unborn.

The Rajahs of Cochin are said to be the lineal descendants of Ceram Perumal's nephews, who on his demise partitioned his large kingdom, for that object of personal aggrandisement which dissipated the conquests of Alexander the Great. The individual and dis-united states so formed were probably further weakened by smaller apportionments, the rulers of which had certainly some slight blood relationship with each other, but not sufficient to curb those jealous feelings of a neighbour's might which brought about constant wars and their attendant miseries. And each sovereign was too short-sighted to comprehend that the humiliation of a rival by a greater power would cause his own insecurity; and so, each was indisposed to lend assistance against a common enemy, and now the Rajah of Cochin, now the Zamorin of

Calicut, or others, enjoyed supremacy by turns, until Tippoo marched his armies into the northern states, and annexed them to his dominions, whilst the Rajahs of Cochin and Travancore took the opportunity to seize the middle and southern.

The Rajah of Cochin, in former days, enjoyed despotic power, of which he delegated a portion to two officers called Karriakars, one of whom acted as Lieutenant of the Northern, the other of the Southern districts of the kingdom. They also appointed deputies under them, for whose acts they were held responsible; and these deputies had their subordinates who came more directly in contact with the people. A species of Feudal System seems to have prevailed in the earliest periods. The lord of small tracts, called Arunatil Probuhkmer, exercised, like the baron of old, a tyrannical rule over his tenants, or vassals, and enforced their assistance in any personal feud with a neighbour, or when the Rajah required their service. He was withheld from acts of oppression or rebellion simply from respect for his sovereign's superior might, which it naturally became the interest of all the chiefs to maintain. With the progress of civilization, and the wider distribution of wealth, the power of these lords became weak, and finally died out, much, doubtless, to the satisfaction of the Rajah.

The Rajah possessed a right over the lives of all his subjects ; and, though he was wisely cautious in its exercise, even Karriakars have had to bow their heads to his displeasure. Fealty to him was not sworn, but assumed with the tenure of land, and we rarely find any instance of the obligation being forgotten. He raised his army by conscription from the Nairs, except when some great emergency required additional forces, and then he even employed Kaffir mercenaries. All castes inferior to the Nairs were liable to be pressed into the service of the army as camp-followers, but they were rarely permitted to join in the fight, as the antagonists were generally raised also from the superior caste, and as a matter of religion, therefore, they should not be opposed by any of low birth. This was a strange system, which reasonably excited the astonishment of the first European settlers, but suited the country well in permitting agriculture, &c. to proceed without much interruption, confining the greatest dangers to a sort of militia, and thus keeping the body of the people numerically strong.

The soil was tilled by slaves, a most debased miserable race, whose progenitors were doubtless those wild aborigines of the hills, who bricked up their aged parents in stone tunnels, and rejoiced in the perpetration of fiendish barbarities. They were sold, mortgaged, and put to death at the will of the owner; and being brought up with a belief in their master's right, and their own individual inferiority, they endured the greatest miseries with callousness. The British Government has declared their fetters broken, and taken much trouble to assure the poor creatures of their absolute freedom; but though some have taken advantage of it, by far the greater number have not comprehended the reform, and are so pliant and miserably ignorant that even now transfers of such live stock are made, *sub rosâ*, with an estate, illegal as are any such transactions. They are mostly employed now, as their ancestors were for centuries, in damming, irrigating, ploughing, sowing, and reaping the paddy fields, in small oases of which they live with hardly a clearer idea of the world beyond the watery plains around than the buffaloes which wallow like themselves in the rich mud of the district. They are compelled to make a by-path among brake and brier, cobras, and scorpions, when approaching the haunts of civilization, and not on any account to use the high road. Their food is of the most loathsome description; their habits brutish; their diseases awful; and their condition in every respect as degraded and miserable as can be imagined. But the glorious light of the Gospel is at length entering their abode; the interest expressed in them by the English Missionaries, at first incomprehensible, has now secured their gratitude, and the plan of salvation, slowly explained, has produced abundant promise of such a harvest as has not yet been gleaned from the semi-educated classes of India.

The slaves, until very recently, had no court to appeal to for redress of any grievances, and this hardship had also to be endured by the low castes when the aggressor was a man of high birth. Justice was nominally administered in accordance with the laws and regulations of the Hindoo sacred books; but might and bribe, caste and creed, also influenced the Judge's decision, and the plaintiff was sometimes tempted to use other and more deadly arguments to satisfy those revengeful feelings which more than any others harass the inhabitant of these parts.

Internal communication appears to have been well kept up by the construction of canals and locks to extend the advantages of the Backwater system. Only few roads were made, whether from lack of ability or perseverance is unimportant; but their want has been at all times felt by the people in the interior, who, doubtless, would endeavour to raise many valuable articles were there a cheap mode of transmitting them to the market.

The Rajah of Cochin has now but little of that authority which his predecessors so long and uselessly exercised. He is a monarch of ancient descent, almost the solitary representative of the great Malabar kings, and the nominal ruler of one of the few kingdoms that Britain has not annexed to her Indian conquests; but his power is merely visionary, and his throne but a seat of honour tolerated under great restrictions by our Government. This gradual decline has resulted chiefly from the debilitating effects of the incessant wars with neighbours, which remaining long unseen during the consequent excitement became painfully apparent when Tippoo, in 1790, threatened to march into the country. An appeal for assistance was made to the East India Company, and was readily afforded by a treaty dated the 6th January 1791, which provided that one lac of rupees should be paid annually as a tribute for the protection of the British Government. But in the beginning of the year 1809 the Rajah attempted to recover his independence, and thereby rendered it incumbent upon the Company to frame a new treaty which should leave him all the insignia of royalty, but transfer all virtual sovereignty to them. As a specimen of those incomparable documents which have effected so many salutary reforms in India, as well as for showing our present relations with the Cochin Government, this latter treaty is given verbatim:—

TREATY of perpetual friendship and subsidy between the Honorable the English East India Company Bahdar and the Rajah of Cochin.

Whereas an agreement was concluded in the year 1790, between the Honorable East India Company Bahdar and the late Rajah of Cochin, by which that Rajah was to be put in possession of, and to hold on specific conditions as a vassal of the Honorable Company, certain Districts therein enumerated.

And whereas the present Rajah, losing sight of the benefits derived to him and to his country from the favor and protection of the Honorable Company, did lately unite himself to the Dewan of Travancore for the prosecution of daring and unprovoked measures of hostility against the said Company.

And whereas it is notorious that the troops of the Rajah aforesaid did continue to act with the Travancore troops, while in hostility to the Honorable Company, for six weeks subsequent to the conclusion of an arrangement made on the 8th of February 1809, by the Resident at Travancore, with the Sirkar of the Rajah of Cochin, whereby the Sirkar aforesaid agreed to separate from its hostile alliance with the Dewan of Travancore; such conduct being manifestly a breach of that engagement, and an aggravation of the former hostile proceedings.

And whereas, notwithstanding these and other acts of hostility and perfidy on the part of the Sirkar of Cochin, the Honorable Company, guided by clemency and moderation, is still willing to re-establish the ancient connection and friendship with the aforesaid Rajah upon the basis of subsisting engagements, but with such modifications as, with the consent of the Rajah aforesaid, shall serve to provide for a reasonable reparation and indemnification for the past, and establish a security for the future.

With these objects in view, the following articles for a new Treaty between the Honorable Company and the Rajah of Cochin have been agreed upon and settled by the Resident of Travancore; Lieutenant-Colonel Colin Macaulay being duly vested with authority thereto by the Honorable Sir George Hilaro Barlow, Baronet, and Knight of the most Honorable Order of the Bath, Governor in Council of Fort St. George, on the part of the Honorable East India Company, and by the Rajah of Cochin for himself and successors, to be binding upon the contracting parties as long as the Sun and Moon shall endure.

ARTICLE I.

The friends and enemies of either of the contracting parties shall be considered as the friends and enemies of both; the Honorable the East India Company Bahdar engaging to defend and protect the territories of the Rajah of Cochin against all enemies whomsoever.

ARTICLE II.

In consideration of the stipulations in the preceding article, the Rajah of Cochin agrees to pay annually to the said Honorable Company a sum equal to the expense of one Battalion of Native Infantry; the amount to be payable in six equal Kists, and the payment to commence from the 1st of May 1809; and it is agreed that the disposal of the said amount, with the distribution of the force to be maintained by it, whether stationed within the territories of the Rajah of Cochin or of the Honorable Company, shall be left entirely to the Company.

ARTICLE III.

Should it become necessary to employ a larger force for the defence and protection of the Cochin territories against foreign invasion than is stipulated for by the preceding article, the Rajah of Cochin agrees to contribute towards the discharge of the increased expense thereby incurred, such a sum as shall appear to the Governor in Council of Fort St. George, on an attentive consideration of the means of the said Rajah, to bear a just and reasonable proportion to the actual net revenue of the said Rajah.

ARTICLE IV.

And whereas it is indispensably necessary that effectual and lasting security should be provided against any failure in the funds destined to defray either the expenses of the permanent military force in time of peace, or the extraordinary expenses described in the third article of the present Treaty, it is hereby stipulated and agreed between the contracting parties that whenever the Governor in Council of Fort St. George shall have reason to apprehend such failure in the funds so destined, the said Governor in Council shall be at liberty, and shall have full power and right, either to introduce such regulations and ordinances as he shall deem expedient for the internal management and collection of the revenues, or for the better ordering of any other branch or department of the Rajah of Cochin, or to assume and bring under the direct management of the servants of the said Company Bahdar such part or parts of the territorial possessions of the Rajah of Cochin as shall appear to him the said Governor in Council necessary to render the funds efficient and available either in time of peace or war.

ARTICLE V.

And it is hereby further agreed that whenever the said Governor in Council shall signify to the said Rajah of Cochin that it is become necessary to carry into effect the provisions of the fourth article, the said Rajah shall immediately issue orders to his Karriakars or other officers either for carrying into effect the said regulations and ordinances, according to the tenor of the fourth article, or for placing the territories required under the exclusive authority and control of the English Company Bahdar; and in case the said Rajah shall not issue such orders within ten days from the time when the application shall have been formally made to him, then the said Governor in Council shall be at liberty to issue orders by his authority, either for carrying into effect the said regulations and ordinances, or for assuming the management and collection of the revenues of the said territories, as he shall judge most expedient for the purposes of securing the efficiency of the said military funds and of providing for the effectual protection of the country and the welfare of the people; provided always, that whenever and so long as any part or parts of the said Rajah's territories shall be placed and shall remain under the exclusive authority and control of the said East India Company, the Governor in Council shall render to the Rajah a true and faithful account of the revenues and produce of the territories so assumed; provided also that in no case whatever shall the said Rajah's actual receipt of annual income arising out of his territorial revenue be less than the sum of thirty-five thousand rupees, together with one-fifth part of the nett revenues of the whole of his territories: which sum of the said thirty-five thousand rupees, together with the amount of one-fifth of the said nett revenues, the East India Company engages at all times and in every possible case to secure and cause to be paid for the use of the said Rajah.

ARTICLE VI.

The Rajah of Cochin engages that he will be guided by a sincere and cordial attention to the relations of peace and amity established between the English Company Bahdar and their allies, and that he will carefully abstain from any interference in the affairs of any state in alliance with the said English Company Bahdar or of any state whatever; and for securing the object of this stipulation it is further stipulated and agreed that no communication or correspondence with any foreign state whatever shall be holden by the said Rajah without the previous knowledge and sanction of the said English Company Bahdar.

ARTICLE VII.

The Rajah of Cochin stipulates and agrees that he will not admit any European foreigners into his service without the concurrence of the English Company Bahdar, and that he will apprehend and deliver to the Company's Government all Europeans of whatever description who shall be found within the territories of the said Rajah without regular passports from the English Government, it being the said Rajah's determined resolution not to suffer, even for a day, any European foreigners to remain within the territories now subjected to his authority, unless by consent of the said Company.

ARTICLE VIII.

Whereas the complete protection of the said Rajah's territories may require that such fortresses as are situated within the said territories should be dismantled or garrisoned, as well as in time of peace as of war, by British troops and officers, the said Rajah hereby engages that the said English Company shall at all times be at liberty to dismantle or garrison, in whatever manner they may judge proper, such fortresses and strong places within the territories of the said Rajah as it shall appear to them advisable to take charge of.

ARTICLE IX.

The Rajah of Cochin hereby promises to pay at all times the utmost attention to such advice as the English Government shall occasionally judge it necessary to offer to him with a view to the accommodation of his finances, the better collection of his revenues, the administration of justice, the extension of commerce, the encouragement of trade, agriculture, and industry, or any other objects connected with the advancement of the interests of the said Rajah, the happiness of his people, and mutual welfare of both states.

ARTICLE X.

This Treaty, consisting of ten articles, being this day, the sixth day of May, 1809, settled and concluded at the palace of Anjekamal, near Cochin, by Lieutenant-Colonel Colin Macaulay, Resident of Travancore, on the one part, on behalf and in the name of the Honourable Sir George Hilaro Barlow, Baronet, and Knight of the most Honourable Order of the Bath, Governor in Council of Fort St. George, on the part of the Honourable English East India Company; and on the other part by the Rajah of Cochin for himself and successors; the Lieutenant-Colonel aforesaid has delivered to the said Rajah one copy of the same in English and Ṭamul signed and sealed by him; and the said Rajah has delivered to the Lieutenant-Colonel aforesaid another copy, also in Tamul and English, bearing his seal and signature; and the aforesaid Lieutenant-Colonel has engaged to procure, and deliver to the said Rajah without delay, a copy of the same under the seal and signature of the Honourable the Governor in Council, on the receipt of which by the said Rajah the present Treaty shall be deemed complete and binding on the Honourable the English East India Company and on the Rajah of Cochin, and the copy of it now delivered to the the said Rajah shall be returned.

By the Honourable the Governor in Council,

(Signed) THE RAJAH OF COCHIN.
G. H. BARLOW.
W. PETRIE.
T. OAKES.
J. H. CASAMAIJOR.

(Signed) A. FALCONAR,
Chief Secretary to Government.

Ratified in Council on the 17th October, 1809.

By the Rt. Honourable the Governor General in Council.

(Signed) MINTO.
G. H. BARLOW.
T. OAKES.
J. H. CASAMAIJOR.

(Signed) A. FALCONAR,
Chief Secretary to Government.

(Compared) JAS. BRITAIN.

The Musnud of Cochin being thus relieved of all dangerous power, and the serious and anxious duties of government being undertaken by another nation, its occupant has apparently but few of those cares which are said to render the slumbers of monarchs uneasy. His Highness RAVEE WURMAH, the present Rajah of Cochin, was born on the 8th February 1828, and on the death of his brother, ascended the throne on the 5th May 1853. His reign, though unfeatured by any extensive reforms, has yet been long enough to convince the British Government of his desire to promote any plans by which the prosperity and happiness of his subjects may be induced. His Highness is tall, slender, and active, with an oval face, sparkling vivacious eyes, and mild expression of countenance. His manners are polite, his habits economical, his disposition benevolent. He reads and talks English with facility, is well informed upon history and the topics of the day, and studies to diffuse knowledge among his subjects. He is, by the inevitable laws of his caste, unmarried, and leads a comparatively solitary life, which varies little from the following arrangement:—He rises a little before six, devotes about an hour to private affairs, then proceeds to the bath, and performs the many tedious ceremonies enjoined on all good Hindoos, which, with prayers at the pagoda, occupy him until ten, at which time he returns to the palace, and breakfasts. The meal consists of nothing but a variety of vegetable curries and rice, served up on plantain leaves. From a little after ten until four, with a slight interval for sweetmeats at noon, he receives, in the audience chamber, such application for office or emolument as is at his disposal, and attends to a few trifling matters that have been left to his own consideration. Riding or driving occupies the hour from four to five, and thence to seven his private affairs. Seven to eight bath, ceremonies, and prayer; then dinner (corresponding exactly to the breakfast), and at half-past eight he retires to rest.

He resides principally at Tripoontrah, a small town about six miles from the capital. The palace and pagoda, which include the main part of the buildings, are unremarkable for any display of costly adornment, but the gateways are interesting blocks of Hindoo architecture, somewhat similar in style (on a small scale) to the elaborate temples at Tanjore. The streets are kept scrupulously clean, and the dust is always sprinkled with cow-dung water when any one of consequence is to pass. The higher castes only are permitted to approach the royal dwelling; and handsome well-fed Bramhans form nearly the entire population of the locality, and are so clean and neat in appearance, and of so fair a colour, that one seems to have been transported among an entirely new and superior nation. The princesses, and their ladies, wear an abundance of snow white muslin around the hips, but no upper garment. The neck is decorated with valuable ornaments, and the ears support very large and beautifully chased pendants. The hair is either worn in a large double knot on the crown, or on the right side of the head, and a band of gold strains it from off the face. The Rajah and all the princes are indistinguishable, in private, from the people around, for their dress consists simply of the muslin round the middle. A body of the Rajah's guards stands sentry before the palace. Their uniform resembles that of our sepoys minutely; high glazed helmet, a small coarse scarlet tail-coat with yellow facings, and white trousers. When His Highness walks or rides out, a guard of honour attends him, and constables, or outriders, clear the way.

The palace at Muttencherry, near Cochin, is used on all state occasions similarly to our St. James's. Its exterior is plain, and the interior hardly more interesting. The audience chamber, a long narrow room, has a few mirrors along the walls, and a rather handsomely carved ceiling; but it is almost unfurnished. On Durbar days arm-chairs covered with red cloth are placed in two rows at right angles to the Rajah's silver seat, which is under a small canopy; the three next to his right hand being occupied by the British Resident, the Elliah Rajah, and the First Prince; and the three next his left hand by the Commander of the Resident's Escort, the Second and Third Princes. The Durbar, or levee, is held upon such occasions as the presentation of a new Resident's credentials, of replies to the Rajah's communications to Government, and the accession to the throne. Invitations are issued two or three days previously in the following form:—

> *At the request of His Highness the Rajah, Mr. Maltby solicits the pleasure of Mr.——'s company at a Public Durbar at the Muttencherry Palace on Monday, the* 13*th Instant, at* 2 P. M.
>
> *Bolghatty,* 11*th February,* 1860.

Civilians in full dress, and the military and those entitled to the distinction in uniform, make their appearance about the hour specified, and are ushered into a small tent, where the plainest of collations is served.

The belted peons, and the silver sticks in waiting, now bustle to the landing place, and make way for His Highness the Elliah Rajah, who, attired in a rich cloth-of-gold tunic and jewelled turban, proceeds to meet the Resident upon his arrival.

This is announced by spasmodic discharges of small field-pieces. Finely painted and costly cushioned palankeens are at once brought up for the great people, and in these they are borne to the foot of a flight of stone steps, at the top of which the Rajah himself waits to welcome the Resident. Together they proceed into the adjoining audience chamber, and are followed by the guests, and a crowd of officious peons, &c. After the usual compliments the Resident intimates that he is the bearer of a letter from Her Majesty's Secretary of State for India, or from the Governor of Madras, to His Highness; and a most clerical-looking individual advances and presents it, wrapped in scarlet silk, upon a gold salver. The Resident then delivers it with a graceful bow to His Highness, who breaks the seal, and reads the contents slowly and carefully. Some short conversation then ensues, and after further bland compliments wreaths of jessamin are brought in, and the Rajah places these around the necks and arms of his visitors, and presents each with a bouquet on which he sprinkles a little exquisite attar of roses from a small gold bottle. He then accepts the Resident's arm, accompanies him to the door, and there shakes hands with him and all his European visitors as they leave the presence. On some occasions the Rajah pays a return visit to the Residency a few days after the Durbar.

At Trichoor and several intermediate towns there are

small palaces, some few of which are plainly furnished, whilst others are nothing more than wayside resting-places for the royal family during a progress through the kingdom.

The ceremony of coronation has been necessarily dispensed with, as, by an old statute, the Rajah must assume the crown at no other place than Ponany, a town of which the Zamorin of Calicut, the Sultan of Mysore, and lastly the British Government, have been the possessors since it was first forfeited by the Cochin monarch. The accession to the throne is signified by a grand Durbar, at which the Resident and all the dignitaries of the realm are, if possible, present. The succession is most singular, for, firstly, the Rajah's children have no interest in it, but those of his sisters have, and, supposing his younger brother is the senior of all his nephews, he becomes Elliah Rajah or heir apparent; but in the case of there being no younger brother, the eldest son of the senior sister becomes Elliah Rajah, and the next to him in age First Prince, and so on. But if the Ranee (the Rajah's eldest sister) had a son, and another brother was subsequently born to the Rajah, the nephew would rank in the line of succession before the uncle, and thus the heir apparent is sometimes a nephew, and the First Prince a brother of the reigning sovereign. If the eldest sister dies without issue, the sons of the eldest surviving one become the presumptive heirs to the crown. The sisters of the Rajah are of lower caste than the Bramhans, but, it being held that the sovereign must have some aristocratic blood in his veins, they are married to men of that caste, who thereby forfeit their rank of birth, but obtain an allowance from the country as a compensation. Their children are called Chetrians. Although the Salic Law prevails so far that the Rance is not allowed to reign, she becomes (in connection with her children) one of the most important personages in the country, and receives all that distinction which is shown elsewhere to a Queen Consort.

The present Royal Family of Cochin consists of the following members:—

H.H. RAVEE WURMAH,	*Rajah of Cochin,*	Born	8th Feb. 1828.
H.H. WALLIA AMAH TAMBOORAN	*Mother of the Rajah,*	"	5th Dec. 1795.
H.H. COONJEE AMAH TAMBOORAN	*Sister of the Rajah,*	"	3rd May, 1814.
H.H. COONJEE PILLAH TAMBOORAN	" "	"	22nd July, 1822.
H.H. COONJEE CAVA TAMBOORAN	" "	"	7th Dec. 1832.
H.H. MUNGOO TAMBOORAN	" "	"	30th Sept. 1839.

NEPHEWS OF THE RAJAH.

H.H. RAMA WURMAH,	*Elliah Rajah of Cochin,*	"	11th May, 1835.
H.H. VEERACARALA WURMAH	*1st Prince of Cochin,*	"	30th Aug. 1845.
H.H. RAMA WURMAH,	*2nd Prince of Cochin,*	"	2nd Jan. 1848.
H.H. VEERACARALA WURMAH	*3rd Prince of Cochin,*	"	13th Feb. 1850.
H.H. RAMA WURMAH,	*4th Prince of Cochin,*	"	27th Dec. 1852.
H.H. RAVEE WURMAH,	*5th Prince of Cochin,*	"	4th Nov. 1853.
H.H. VEERACARALA WURMAH	*6th Prince of Cochin,*	"	9th Sept. 1854.
H.H.	*7th Prince of Cochin,*	"	2nd Oct. 1859.

AND NINE NIECES OF THE RAJAH.

There is little probability of the extinction of this family for many years. On a few occasions such a circumstance has happened in the history of Cochin, and recourse been had to adoption from two other families distantly connected with that on the throne. A special provision requires that no person of lower caste than the Nairs shall at any time reign.

The ordinary allowance to the Rajah for his private expenses is about 5,500 *rs.* per mensem; to his mother and sisters 1,000 *rs.*; to the Elliah Rajah 500 *rs.*; and to the First Prince 250 *rs.*; further grants are sometimes made for special occasions. The Rajah has saved a handsome sum of money, and invested it (with a balance of the revenue of about nine or ten lacs) in E. I. Co.'s paper. His mother too has a large interest in British solvency.

The Rajah of Cochin is responsible for all his actions to our Government. Titles of honour and promotions proceed from him, but it is expected that the nomination of the Dewan or Prime Minister shall be only made with the approval of the Resident. The privilege of mercy towards criminals is permitted, but with certain restrictions which much diminish the power. A small silver coin called *puttans* (of which 19¼ equal a rupee) are coined at his command, but on no regular or extensive plan, British-minted money being almost universally used. His relations have no share in power, neither is the Heir Apparent permitted to take a seat in the Council. He can appoint them to lucrative sinecures, but an impression that it would be considered derogatory to their rank hinders them from accepting office. His training in youth is consequently inefficient in experiencing him early in the government of the country; but from his English tutor he acquires some idea of the language, manners, customs, and character of his supporters; and from his Bramhan preceptor he learns the profound schemes of Hindooism, the necessity of constant purification from outward defilement by systematic ablutions, and the call upon him to support and benefit that high caste of which he, the Rajah, is not and can never be an equal. His education is therefore calculated to make him wisely abstain from any interference with us; and by this system alone—by relinquishing for ever the hope of recovering his independence, by profiting by the lesson taught by the late unsuccessful mutiny, and by assisting the British Government in its endeavours to promote the civilisation, prosperity, and happiness of his subjects, the Rajah of Cochin will, it is hoped, long remain one of our most faithful and constant allies.

The revenue of Cochin does not vary very much from about nine lacs per annum. It is derived chiefly from a land-tax, which is assessed once in twelve years according to the crops and condition of the ground; and from monopolies of tobacco, pepper, cardamoms, and salt. The Dewan possesses the right to impose further taxes, but for a long period no need has been felt to take advantage of it, as the land is being so widely planted with the tax-paying cocoa-nut tree, that deficiency in one source of income has been fully repaired by an increase, more especially in returns on account of such plantations. The Rajah in former times used to take what he wanted, upon a verbal understanding of accounting for the loan on some distant day, the arrival of which, it may be guessed, was not a wise subject of conversation to a despotic monarch; but now he receives the fixed allowance, and transfers the entire care of the exchequer to his Dewan. This minister has, consequently, great influence in the country, and it is according to his character rather than to the Rajah's that national prosperity results. The balance at the credit of Cochin in British bonds was almost wholly saved by Shungra Warrier, the penultimate Dewan, an able, upright man, whose eldest son, Shungoony Menon, has just been appointed to this distinguished office amid universal satisfaction.

The body guard of the Rajah numbers about three hundred men. There is no special tax for its maintenance, but a small allowance made monthly from the revenue towards that object. It is under the control of the Dewan, and is generally quartered at Tripoontrah. It is raised by voluntary enlistment, and no lack of recruits is ever found, as the service is light and the pay considerable.

Before 1833 justice was administered without any written law, but at that date the statutes of the E. I. Co. were compiled for the use of the judges. High treason, murder, manslaughter, robbery, burglary, theft, &c., are punished in accordance with our own regulations, excepting that transportation cannot be sentenced for want of colonies; and so the convicts remain in the country and repair roads, build bridges, &c., in gangs, under the surveillance of armed peons. Judgment for capital offences cannot be executed without the approval of the Resident. There are no public prosecutors; but the plaintiff makes out his charge, and after he has been sworn, the prisoner conducts his own defence. Oaths are administered with a careful consideration of what is most binding upon different creeds, and no opportunity is allowed for perjury by a subsequent statement that the affirmation was not obliging upon the conscience. The trial commences with the assumption of the prisoner's innocence, but his confession of guilt sways the proceedings.

The Courts of Law consist of an Appeal and Zillah Court at Ernaccollum (near Cochin), and a Zillah Court at Trichoor; whilst half a dozen Tassildars are stationed in different districts to hear and dispose of petty offences. If, however, the case is very serious, they send it up to the criminal section of the Zillah Courts, of which there are two Judges (one a Christian) and a Hindoo law officer, called a Shastry. Here it is judged, or committed to the Circuit Court, and thence (if of a very grave character) to the Appeal Court. Claims of a civil nature are preferred, at first, to one of the Zillah Courts; but dissatisfaction with the judgment there obtained permits of recourse to the Appeal Court, whose opinion is final.

Such is the country over which the Rajah is the nominal ruler. It owes its very individuality to Britain, and can only retain it for the time to come by faithful adhesion to the articles of the Treaty of 1806. Its history in connexion with ours is most interesting; and the progress made in the last few years in supplying Europe with some valuable commodities, and the ascertained capability of the soil to produce abundantly of other staples, afford the best promise of its future being prosperous. But the system of monopoly must give way to principles of free trade before any great improvement can be effected; and in anticipation of more attention being given to so necessary a reform, the recent change of the Rajah's advisers has been viewed with much interest by all his well-wishers.

NATIVE COCHIN.

CHAPTER VII.

THE JEWS.

Signs indicating the speedy restoration of the Jews—Interest attached to their history—Early settlement of a large body at Cranganore—Portuguese persecution — Tolerant consideration by the Dutch—Parentage, character, and peculiarities of the White and Black Jews—Celebration of Feasts—Style of Dress—Means of livelihood—Rites and ceremonies—Prophecies relating to the people—Their fulfilment.

Wars and rumours of wars, revolutions and disorganizations of society, the extinction of Papal dominion, the impending destruction of Mohammedanism, and the preaching of the Gospel to every nation, are signs that those times are rapidly approaching when the "Divine indignation against the Jews is to be accomplished," and they collectively are to "return to their own land." Independently of this expectation, they are the most interesting people in the world: they are associated with the first knowledge acquired in childhood, with the most pious thoughts of the Divine, and the most anxious fears of the merchant; their vitality, in spite of persecution and with no visible head, is as astonishing as their acquirement of almost absolute power over the civilised world by the influence of their enormous wealth and credit. Notwithstanding their dispersion, they have retained the hope of their speedy re-establishment as a nation in Palestine; not as an idle tradition, like that of the Russians, who anticipate their Czar's universal sovereignty, but explicable as the most prominent tenet of their own and their ancestors' faith. In Europe, experience of the advantage of assimilating their costume and outward manners to the fashion of people around, has induced them to relinquish many peculiarities that formerly distinguished them in a crowd; and though his physiognomy sometimes indicates his parentage, it is not now very easy to point out the Jew. But in India the pure descendant of the children of Israel is at once discerned by the singularity of his costume and—what is far more remarkable—his fair complexion; and in Cochin a small community is thus immediately discovered. Its history is not more free from suffering incident than that of the wanderers in other lands; but upon some points it is peculiarly interesting, and worthy of more attention than has hitherto been shown it.

From the native annals of Malabar and their own traditions, it appears that ten thousand Jews arrived on the coast about A.D. 70, shortly after the destruction of the second Temple and the final desolation of Jerusalem. It is supposed that some seven thousand settled at once on a spot then called Mahodranpatna, but now Cranganore, and applied themselves, with their usual sagacity, economy, and success, to trade, and thence early obtained the respect and protection of the native princes. Some considerable time afterwards they procured a most valuable grant from the ruling sovereign, and had it engraved in Malayalim upon a copper plate. This plate is still in existence; a small insignificant-looking thing, with rudely scratched letters of such an old-fashioned character that little resemblance can be traced to those now in use. A translation of it was made some years ago, but the Jews are not quite agreed upon the meaning of some words, and can only settle its date about A.D. 500, according to some very old traditions. Many suppose that the renowned CERAM PERUMAL was the donor, as the attestation is right royal; and if that is a right conjecture, the date to be assigned to the grant should be about A.D. 750, when he appears to have been in the zenith of his power. It is undoubtedly a thousand years old, and exceedingly interesting, not only for its proving the high consideration in which the Jews were held, but also for showing what honours and privileges were then considered valuable. The following is a translation from a Malayalim manuscript rendering of the original Hebrew interpretation of the copper plate:—

"To that God, who of His almighty will and pleasure created this world and its Kings, I, ERAVY VIRMA, lift up my hands in adoration, and bestow this grant, as from time immemorial our sovereignty has existed, at Cranganore, on this day of the thirty-sixth year of our reign; and by this I do hereby ordain and give all manner of powers to JOSEPH RABBAN, to wear of five different colours, to be saluted by the firing of guns, to ride on elephants and horses, to have an herald on the roads, to make converts of five nations, to have the lamp of the day, to walk upon carpets spread upon the ground, to adorn his house, to use palankeens, high parasols, kettle drums, trumpets, and small drums; and, to all these privileges. I grant freedom from ground-rent and duty to seventy-two families, and appoint him Chief and Governor of the Houses of Congregation. All the above-cited privileges are hereby, without the least difference or contradiction, fully granted by this copper plate unto the said JOSEPH RABBAN, his heirs, male and

female, brides and bridegrooms, to hold and exercise, as long as they may be in this world. May God grant His blessing to the under-mentioned witnesses.

"King BIVADA CUBERTIN MITADIN, and he is King of Travancore.

"King AIRLA NADA MANA VIKRIIN, and he is the Samorin King.

"King VELODA NADA ARCHRIN SHATEN, and he is King of Argot.

"King BIDDATAROO COADDA, and he is King of Palgatchery.

"King IROY BILLAPANTA, and he is King of Colastri.

"King MOODACAN CHATTEN, and he is King of Carbinah.

"King WAJACHERY KANDAN, and he is King of Varachangur.

"Written by Kellapen.

"As the Cochin Rajah PEREMPAHDAPPA is my heir, his name is not included in this."

Dr. Claudius Buchanan was informed that the community at Cranganore was increased by an emigration of Jews from Spain, Judea, and other parts; and that the Colony continued to flourish until discord unhappily sprung up, and the assistance of an Indian King was called in by one party to reduce that opposed to it; and that the King besieged the place, destroyed the houses and strongholds, dispossessed the people, put some to death, and carried others away into captivity; whilst a few managed to escape, and obtained an asylum from the Rajah of Cochin. But from subsequent enquiry the Portuguese appear to have been the oppressors in the case.

Mr. Moens, Governor of Cochin in 1773, mentions that some internal commotion had weakened the strength of the Jews at Cranganore previous to the arrival of the Portuguese; and for this reason, it is probable, the Europeans found easy access into the port. But they soon lost the regard of their new dependants by their intolerance and bigotry, and about, it is supposed, A.D. 1565 the Jews fled to Cochin and sued for the Rajah's protection. He, with a liberality that can hardly be understood, granted them a small piece of ground at the side of his palace, and on this they built a little town. The Portuguese, however, continued their persecution, robbed, beat, and drove away any whom they met; whilst the officials would afford them no redress whatever. It was only natural, therefore, that the Jews should hail the arrival of the Dutch with joy, and endeavour to afford them every assistance; for which, after the first unsuccessful attack, the Portuguese revenged themselves most cruelly. But the Dutch shortly appeared again, and captured the town; and, with a recollection of their former services, granted the Jews many privileges, and traded with them. They have never yet recovered from their misfortunes at Cranganore, but seem to bewail the loss of their former wealth and power, without feeling any energy to strive to recover either.

The Cochin Jews are divided into two distinct classes, one known as the Jerusalem, or White, the other as the Black Jews. The former are the descendants of the first settlers by marriage *solely* with one another. Their complexion is not exactly European, but it is the pale olive freshness most nearly allied to it, and the delicate carnation of the tips of the fingers proves that no native blood flows in their veins. Their features are fine, if not (especially with the elders) noble; broad and high forehead, roman nose, thick lips, generally however concealed by a most luxuriant, jet-black, curly beard. The women, when young, have mostly a Spanish style of face, though in a few cases the pale-coloured hair, and light brown or blue eyes, would induce the idea of a more northern parentage. They are rather short, and from their mode of costume and inelegance of gait are not remarkable for any other charms than that of a face which for contour and expression may be called truly beautiful. But whilst the Jew seems to improve in appearance as years creep on, the Jewess "fades as the leaf fades," and at thirty years of age is plainness itself. The children look almost leprously white, so habituated does the eye become in India to dark skins. This retention of complexion and features for so many centuries is truly astonishing, when it is considered that the descendants of the Portuguese are generally of a *darker* hue than even the aborigines of the country. It furnishes the strongest argument against any idea that the sun darkens the skin; and also seems to warrant some hope that the colonization of India *may* be effected if Europeans would only marry Europeans.

The Black Jews may either be the descendants of early native proselytes, or of individuals entitled to a *bar sinister*. Some few of them have a Hebrew cast of countenance, but by far the greater number are indistinguishable from the natives around. They are considered by the White Jews as an inferior race,- not of *pure* caste, and intermarriage between them never, consequently, takes place. Their customs, forms of prayer, songs, &c., are the same as those of the White Jews, but they do not observe the same strict Levitical ceremonies, and having no legitimate relationship with Hebrews in other lands, they are considered, and pride themselves upon being, a distinct sect.

The White Jews profess to be of the sect of the Pharisees, but are unable to name the tribe to which they belong. This is not to be wondered at, as the very existence of the tribes is involved in much obscurity; and though some believe that the tribes are to be traced, more especially, in the countries of their first captivity, the conjecture seems fruitless, as the object of dividing the Israelites into families was accomplished when the genealogy of the Messiah was traced to David and Judah. They do not feel that strong active hope which their brethren in Europe are never without of speedily returning to their own land. They firmly believe that at *some* future period they are to return, but state that none but the Almighty knows the time, and, therefore, it is idle to speculate upon its approach; and when any disposition is shown to enter into an argument about the chief tenets of their faith, and to show proofs of the Divine origin of Christianity, they listen for a little while, and then decline further conversation on the plea of inferiority of ability. Yet with this singular apathy about points which are daily and minutely considered by the Jews in Europe, they undoubtedly have a spark within them which would be blown into a flame on their hearing a rumour of the fulfilment of their expatriation; and owing to the nomadic habits of some of their brethren they will be informed of it almost immediately after the first movement is made.

The Jews rise at about five o'clock, and after prayer and ablutions proceed to the synagogue for public devotion. At seven they return home, breakfast, set about the day's business, dine between twelve and two, and again assemble for half an hour's prayer at three;

resume their work until six, when once again they attend the synagogue for about half an hour, and at nine retire to bed. This is the routine of their week-days. On Friday the evening prayer commences at half-past five, and concludes at half-past six, and the Talmud or some other religious work is read until bed time. On Saturday the morning prayer continues from six till nine o'clock, the afternoon from three till four, and the evening, as usual, from six till half-past, with the termination of which they close the Sabbath. They are very exemplary in their observance of this division of time, and rigidly correct in their respect for the seventh day.

The great feasts of the Passover, Pentecost, and Tabernacles are celebrated with the most exact attention to the ritual. The last is observed by the erection of cadjan sheds in the streets, and by a small illumination of the houses with little cups of oil on either side of the doors and windows. Handsome glass chandeliers are suspended from the ceiling of the synagogue, and brazen lamps fixed into the walls; the seats are covered with scarlet cloth, and the Books of the Law are brought out from the recess in which they are usually kept, and displayed in their bright silver cases upon a small stage immediately before the reading desk. The people now flock in, the women ascending into a screened gallery over the entrance, and the men finding room in the body of the building. The dresses of the latter are very handsome; robes of silk, velvet, or satin of a scarlet, blue, green, or amber tint, with costly shawls wrapped around the head and waist, and a lavish display of gold chains and buttons made of English sovereigns. One is reminded immediately of Rubens' superb delineations of the Pharisees; there is the same manly form, fine countenance, and luxuriant beard, the same brilliant and costly dress, and almost precisely the same *style* of dress as he delighted to represent. Their costume does not at all resemble that of the natives of India, and as the Jews say that it is the same as worn by their ancestors, there is reason to imagine, therefore, that it affords a correct idea of the dress of their sect at the commencement of the Christian era.

The service commences with a chant and prayer; a portion of Scripture is then read, or rather intoned, by the officiating Rabbi (who wears the Tallith or veil over his turban), and the impressive silent prayer follows. The people stand in groups facing the Books of the Law, and, with a constant flexion of the body and an occasional low prostration, hum the petitions very rapidly, and apparently with deep consideration. After some minutes the Rabbi gives the initiative, and they burst forth into a tumultuous, if not irreverent chant; in performing which they distort their faces with zeal to make themselves heard. After a further pause the men proceed by turns to the end of the building, and with much show of respect kiss the silver cases enclosing the Books; the women then descend, and go through the same ceremony with most touching solemnity. The service concludes shortly after they have made this solitary annual appearance in the body of the synagogue.

On ordinary occasions the Jews wear a white cotton skull-cap, jacket, waistcoat, and trousers. The jacket has full sleeves, breast pockets, and twelve bright silver buttons, which are fastened in by a fine silver chain attached to the topmost hole. The Jewesses have lately taken a fancy to very sparely-made gowns, of either silk, linen, or chintz, but some years ago their costume was very different, and far more pleasing. They are not often seen out of their little town, but appear content with the relaxation of standing at the doors of their houses whilst embroidering caps or making lace, in which they are singularly expert.

The White Jews, with but a few exceptions, have no very regular or lucrative occupation. At one time they used to import muslins, millinery, and perfumes from Calcutta; but this trade has gradually been taken out of their hands, and they now earn a livelihood by collecting hides in the interior, making casks for sale, and book-binding. They are considered to be rather successful in the last profession, and, with most rude tools, they do certainly bind in a style far better adapted to the climate than any one of the brilliantly decorated exteriors of the London publications. The Black Jews employ themselves as sawyers, carpenters, masons, and one or two as produce merchants. A very few of both classes are sufficiently well off to be enabled to lend money; but the Jews of Cochin, as a body, are miserably poor and uninfluential in the trade and prosperity of the place.

The rite of circumcision is performed here, as elsewhere, on the eighth day after birth. As soon as the child is old enough he is sent to one of the two Rabbis, appointed by the congregation for the purpose, and taught the rudiments of religion, the Hebrew prayers, and a small amount of general information. At thirteen, it is held, his parents or guardians are released from their accountableness for his sins, and on the day succeeding his arrival at that age he is with much solemnity invested with the phylacteries, which he is thenceforward to bind round his head and left arm during his week-day morning devotions. At eighteen he usually marries, having been betrothed some six or twelve months previously, to a girl perhaps five years his junior. Before taking a house, he nails on to the door-post, or scoops out a groove therein and inserts, a small tube in which he has placed some portions of Scripture inscribed most carefully upon fine leather. He and all his friends, on entering or leaving the house, are bound to kiss the tube, or Mazuzah, either with the lips or through the instrumentality of the fingers; and on relinquishing his tenancy he is forbidden to remove it, unless he knows that a Gentile is to succeed him. He employs either poor Hindoos or Christians as domestic servants, on account of the inability of any one of his own faith to prepare food on the Sabbath; and if not able to procure this assistance, he uses a quantity of vinegar in making the Saturday's provision on Friday afternoon, and thus preserves it fresh and wholesome.

When the Jew falls sick and feels the approach of death, he sends urgently for a few friends, confesses his sins aloud, devises his property, arranges for his funeral, and entreats the assistance of their prayers for his soul. The burial takes place three hours after death, unless the relations have to come from far, in which case it is postponed two hours. The funeral is attended by all kinsfolk and acquaintance, as the Jews consider that one of the most benevolent acts to be performed for a friend is to follow him to the grave. The cemetery (called "Beth Harum," or the *House of the Living*) is a little distance behind the town, in the heart of a dense cocoa-nut plantation. The tombs are very numerous, all designed with much care, and three or four of imposing size. The chilly atmosphere of the spot in the evening, the unbroken solitude, the parallel arrangement of the tombs with their feet pointing to the *west*, and the tropical vegetation around, are calculated to impress a stranger with thoughts of the most profound character.

* "There are three remarkable prophecies concerning the Jews:

> The children of Israel shall abide many days without a king, and without a prince, and without a sacrifice, and without an image, and without an ephod, and without teraphim. Hosea III. 4.
>
> The Lord shall scatter thee among all people, from the one end of the earth even unto the other, and lo! the people shall dwell alone, and shall not be reckoned among the nations. Deut. XXVIII. 64, *and* Num. XXIII. 9.
>
> Thou shalt become an astonishment, a proverb, and a byword among all nations whither the Lord shall lead thee. Among these nations shalt thou find no ease, neither shall the sole of thy foot have rest. Deut. XXVIII. 37. 65.

"The first of these prophecies is very remarkable; for whoever heard of a nation 'abiding many days' without its civil and religious polity, and surviving its political existence? The very assertion seems to involve an absurdity. Did the Egyptians, Chaldeans, Greeks, or Romans survive *their* civil and religious polity? The second prediction is not less singular than the former; for if the Jews were to be received among the nations of

* This consideration of the prophecies in connection with the History of the Jews has been extracted from Buchanan's *Christian Researches*, as the Author feels its simplicity will secure it more attention than any comments he might make upon so deeply interesting a subject.

the earth, why should they not 'be reckoned with the nations?' Would any man in a remote age venture to foretel that there was a certain nation which, in the ages to come, would be received and tolerated by all nations, merely to be persecuted? But the third prophecy is such as must afford a contemplation to infidelity to the end of time. The Jews were to become 'an astonishment, and a proverb, and a byword among all the nations,' because they shed the blood of the Saviour of the world. Now it is not surprising that Christians should reproach them for such a crime. But how should we expect that they would be 'trodden down of the *heathen* world,' who never heard of such a Saviour? Behold the Hindoo, at this day punishing the Jew without knowing the crime of which he has been guilty! These three prophecies have been manifestly fulfilled; and if we had no other evidence, this is sufficient to prove 'that there is a God, and that he hath made a revelation to man.'

"There is a fourth prophecy concerning this people which is hastening to its accomplishment. The Prophet Hosea, after foretelling that the children of Israel should abide many days without a King, adds these words:

> Afterwards they shall return, and seek the Lord their God, and David their King; and shall fear the Lord and his goodness in the latter days. Hosea III. 5.

"The question which is now in the mouth of every Christian is that which was asked in the vision by the Prophet Daniel on the same subject: 'How long shall it be to the end of these wonders?' 'When shall the indignation against the holy people be accomplished?' that they may 'return and seek the Lord their God, and David their King.'

"To Daniel the Prophet and to John the Evangelist was given a revelation of the great events of the general Church to the end of time. Daniel foretels that the Christian Church shall be oppressed by the persecuting powers for *a time, times, and the dividing of a time* (Dan. vii. 25). The same period he assigns for the accomplishment of the indignation against the holy people Israel.

> One said, how long shall it be to the end of these wonders? And I heard the man clothed in linen, which was upon the waters of the river, when he held up his right hand and his left hand unto heaven, and sware by Him that liveth for ever, that it shall be for a *time, times, and an half:** and when He shall have accomplished to scatter the power of the holy people, all these things shall be finished. Dan. XII. 6, 7.

"The same form of words is used in the Revelation of St. John to express the duration of the Papal and Mohammedan powers. Oppressed by them, the Church of Christ was to remain desolate in the wilderness for *a time and times, and half a time* (Rev. xii. 14). Every one who is erudite in sacred prophecy will understand that this great period of Daniel and St. John commences at the same era, namely, the rise of the persecuting powers, and that its duration is 1260 years.

"Our blessed Saviour has not left an event of this importance without notice:

> *The Jews* shall be led away captive into all nations; and Jerusalem shall be trodden down of the Gentiles, until the times of the Gentiles be fulfilled. Luke XXI. 24.

"What these 'times of the Gentiles' are, our Lord has explained in his subsequent Revelation to St. John:

* A time, times, and half a time, or a year, two years, and half a year; or forty-two months; or 1260 prophetical days.

> The Court which is without the temple is given unto the Gentiles; and the holy city shall they tread under foot forty and two months. Rev. xi. 2.

"The Apostle Paul has also recorded this event:

> I would not, brethren, that ye should be ignorant of this mystery that blindness, in part, is happened to Israel, until the fulness of the Gentiles be come in; and so all Israel shall be saved. Rom. xi. 25, 26.

"The fulness of time for the conversion of the Gentiles will be come in, when the Papal and Mohammedan obstructions are removed. Such events as the fall of the Pope in the West, and of Mohammed in the East, both of whom persecuted the Jews to death, will probably be the means of awakening the Jews to consider the evidences of that religion which predicted the rise and fall of both.

"But the grand prophecy of the Apostle Paul on this subject is that which respects the *consequence* of the conversion of the Jews. 'The receiving of the Jews,' saith he, 'what shall it be to the world but *life from the dead?*' (Rom. xi. 15.) Dispersed as they are in all countries, and speaking the language of all countries, they would form a body of preachers ready prepared; and they need only say, 'Behold the Scriptures of God in our possession; read our history there as foretold three thousand years ago, and read the events in the annals of nations. We are witnesses to the world and the world to us. Let the whole race of mankind unite and examine the fact!'

> All ye inhabitants of the world, and dwellers on the earth, see ye, when the Lord lifteth up an Ensign on the mountains, and when He bloweth a trumpet, hear ye. Isaiah xviii. 3.

"Thus will their preaching be to the world 'life from the dead.'

"But if the conversion of Israel is to take place when the Papal and Mohammedan powers have fallen (and who does not see that these events are near at hand?) it might be expected that some signs of conciliation between Jews and Christians would now begin to be visible, and is not this the fact? Christians in all countries begin to consider that the indignation against the holy people is nearly accomplished. Many events declare it. The indignation of man is relaxing. The prophecies have been fulfilled regarding it. The GREAT CRIME at CALVARY has been punished by all nations; and we now hear the words of the Prophet addressing us:"

> Comfort ye, comfort ye my people, saith your God, speak ye comfortably to Jerusalem, and cry unto her, that her warfare is accomplished, that her iniquity is pardoned. Isaiah XL. 1.

NATIVE COCHIN.

CHAPTER VIII.

THE LANGUAGE, &c.

Relationship of the languages of South India to Sanscrit—General characteristics of the members of the Dravidian Family—Hindoostani useful, but Malayalim more essential in Cochin—Its cultivation only recent—Little native literature—Proverbs—Diffusion of inestimable knowledge by missionary agency—Computation of time—Local and useful currency—Weights and measures.

The origin of the languages of South India has been traced so convincingly to the same source, that they have lately been classed together into one family, called the Dravidian. It has been supposed that they are all derived from the Sanscrit, the language of the Bramhans, who extended their government from the North to Cape Comorin; but this cannot be. They are indebted for their polish, the expression of abstract notions and moral sentiments, to that tongue truly, but all words employed in ordinary conversation have no connection whatever with it. The further we proceed south the less use is made of Sanscrit derivatives, and the more difficult does it become to trace the former influence of the Bramhans by the discovery of words indicating those profound enquiries, the precursors of social refinement; and thus a very interesting argument is furnished against the, not unusual, conjecture that the civilization of the world commenced from Ceylon as a centre.

The Dravidian family comprises the Tamul, Teloogoo, Canarese, Malayalim, and several others less cultivated. The Tamul is spoken throughout the plain of the Carnatic; the Teloogoo along the Eastern coast from Pulicat to Chicacole, and inland as far as Mysore; the Carnatic throughout Mysore and the Canara district; the Malayalim along the Malabar coast from Mangalore south to Cape Comorin, and inland to the Ghauts. The ground-work of these languages is so very similar that a familiar acquaintance with one renders the acquirement of any other in the same family comparatively easy, and many words are common to all. The natives about Madras find they can sometimes express themselves in a comprehensible manner to the people on this coast; and, in any case, experience little difficulty in picking up the necessary words. These languages have been only lately cultivated, simply from the contempt of the Bramhans for the dialects of their subjects; and any native literature that does exist in these parts is so much sprinkled with Sanscrit illustrations, that one can discern the caste of the writer as easily as the traces of the Norman conquest in our own tongue.

In the town of Cochin a knowledge of Hindoostani is very useful, as the Shroffs are all from the Bombay Presidency, and the produce dealers find it necessary to familiarise themselves with this language. It is also the mother tongue of the better class of domestic servants who do not belong to the district, and of many others in the place. But out of the Fort a knowledge of Malayalim is absolutely necessary in travelling, collecting and preparing produce, &c.; so some few notices of its peculiarities may not be considered out of place in a description of this part of India.

Malayalim is read from left to right like the European languages. Its alphabet consists of fifty-three letters, of which sixteen are vowels, and thirty-seven consonants. The latter contain five gutturals, five palatals, five cerebrals, five dentals, five labials, four semi-vowels, five sibilants, and three other letters that cannot be classed among either of these divisions. There are eight cases of Nouns, viz., the Nominative, Genitive, Dative, Accusative, Vocative, Locative, and two Ablatives; and five Declensions, determined by the formation of the Nominative case. The Pronouns are Personal, Interrogative, and Demonstrative, but no Relative. Hence arises one of the most singular idiomatic peculiarities of the language, viz., the continual and varied use of the Participles, of which there are two kinds, the verbal, and the adjectival formed by inflection from the verbal. Thus,

He shall be like a tree that bringeth forth his fruit in his season:

is thus rendered in Malayalim:

In his season fruit giving a tree like he shall be.

Again, "*St. Matthew's Gospel*" is translated literally, "*St. Matthew having written Gospel*;" where *having written* is an adjectival participle qualifying *Gospel*, but at the same time taking the nomination of the agent.

The Verbs are classed into Transitive, Intransitive, Causal, and Passive. They are formed from neuter nouns, from simple substantives, with the assistance of the verbs *to do, to make*, and from other sources. The conjugation is exceedingly regular, and no inflection is needed to indicate number or person in any but the imperative mood. This exception is interesting. In speaking to persons of low caste, the root of the verb is considered sufficient; but in addressing individuals of high rank, the verbal noun is used for the second person singular, and other modes of expressing deferential respect are not wanting.

Instead of Prepositions the Malayalim language has Postpositions, many of which follow the Nominative case. This is attributed to their existence originally either as nouns, or verbal participles; thus *through Jesus Christ* is translated *Yasu Christhu mulam*, where *mulam* is actually a noun that formerly signified "*root*," "*origin*," "*cause*," and the phrase really means *Jesus Christ being the root.* Again, *he reads with spectacles* is translated *spectacles with he reads*, or yet more correctly, *spectacles having taken he reads*, for the postposition, which we construe by our preposition *with* or *by*, is really the participle of a verb meaning *to have possession of.*

The subordinate phrases in a sentence are almost universally expressed by a repetition of the verbal participles; as,

> Go and wash your face, look in the glass to see that you are clean, and then you may come,

is thus translated:—

> Having gone, your face having washed, in the glass having looked, that you are clean having seen, then you may come.

The researches of Rawlinson, Caldwell, and Norris have been most valuable in discovering a not very remote connexion between the Dravidian and ancient Scythian languages, and Mr. Norris has been especially fortunate in proving that the Scythic portion of the Behistan tablets (written by Darius Hystaspes) show the same peculiarities as have lately been found in the dialects of South India. When it is remembered that we, through our Anglo-Saxon descent, are indebted for the greater part of our language to the Goths (who were undoubtedly Scythians), it may be conjectured that some few traces of a common origin may be traced between English and Malayalim. There are necessarily idiomatic differences so wide that the similarities are not so frequent as to be self-apparent; but the absence of the mood, and the frequent use of the auxiliary verbs in both are remarkable; and considering the many phases through which our language has passed, such remote affinities as the following are not uninteresting:—

It, *itha:* one, *onna;* all (Saxon yeall), *yellan;* stall, *sthallum;* wander, *wanna;* am, *arm;* are, *eyah;* man, *manushen;* papa, *appa;* mamma, *amma.*

Many nouns in English are formed from adjectives and verbs by adding *th*, and yet the active character of the verb is preserved; as, *die, death; four, fourth; grow, growth; true, truth;* &c.; and so in Malayalim *tha* is added to adjectives and participles to substantive them; as, *walla (good), wallatha (the good),* &c.

It has been deemed impossible to express the sounds of the language correctly in Roman type, and consequently the subjoined version of the Lord's prayer will only afford a *general* idea of the pronunciation:—

Swoorgatillulavenayah nyangalooday pedhahvay, ninday namum shoodahmarkaperdernamay; ninday rajeum warernamay, ninday ishtum swoorgatillay polay, bhoomeeyelum cheyaperdernamay; ngangalooday dewasamoollahuppum eenna ngangulka tararnamay, ngangalooday nayray koottum cheyyoonaverooduh ngangul chemekunada polay ngangalooday koottangalay, ngangalordoom chemikayrhamay; ngangoolay pareechayeleyka agaperdootathay; ngangoolay dorshattilninna retchshikeyenamay; endoocondenal rajeawoom, shakteyoom, mahatturvoom, yenaykoom ninakoolladolohagoonada.

Malayalim was never cultivated with any care before the present century. The native literature comprises a few poor translations from Sanscrit writings, and a book entitled "Kerala Uppala," or "Account of Malabar," which treats of many matters from a very early period until the days of Ceram Perumal. The boat songs, and the recitatives in the native drama (which can alone be considered under the head of poetry) are extempore, and most uninteresting productions. There are a few proverbs in general use; the following are given as specimens:—

"It is folly to burn your house in order to destroy the rats."

"Place flowers in your empty cash-box."

"A bride will sweep even the roof, but the old wife will not clean the floor."

"A tired man is uncourteous."

"Roof your house before thatching the porch."

"Pawn not the knife you work with."

"He is the best judge of a dish whose hands reared the herbs."

"The mean man ennobled will display his pomp at midnight."

"A willing gift is doubly valued."

"Plant in prosperity, and so reap in adversity."

"Politeness to the rude is as lines drawn in a stream of water."

"The shoot of a tree can be snapped with the finger, but an axe is required to sever the trunk."

"A poor man's opinion is seldom respected."

"Milk is poison for snakes and grass is milk for cows."

"The value of an eye is understood when it is lost."

"As a golden chain in the hands of a monkey, so is sweet music in the ears of a buffalo."

The first Malayalim Grammar was published by Mr. Drummond in 1799. It has been long out of print, and is now nearly forgotten. It was followed by another, by Mr. Spring; but this also had a limited circulation, and has died out since the Rev. Joseph Peet, of the Church Missionary Society, gave to the world, in 1841, his "Grammar of the Malayalim Language." It has most deservedly passed through several editions, and after a lapse of nigh twenty years is still most highly esteemed, and in general use. The ability required to compose so important a book, and the unceasing attention necessary to improve the revisions, are in themselves worthy of great respect; but when it is considered that thousands have acquired a knowledge of the language solely from this work, that the success of the Church and other Missionary Societies in these parts has been most intimately connected with its study; and that the civilisation and happiness of the people has from that success been most surely promoted, it is not easy to calculate the debt South India, more especially, is under to such a man as Mr. Peet.

The diffusion of useful knowledge by the Malayalim Printing Presses has been most extensive. The German Missionaries have one at Tellicherry, and the Rajah of Travancore has another at Trevandrum; but it is from the Cottayam Church Mission Press that all the books in this district have emanated.

Cottayam C. M. P. was founded by the Rev. J. Bailey, A.D. 1823, and finished in the following year. He then built up a press according to a description in an Encyclopædia, and shortly afterwards received from Bombay —by order of Claudius Buchanan—a small fount of

Malayalim type, with which he first printed "A Charge to the Syrian Churches, by Mar. Athanasius," and subsequently a translation of the fifth chapter of St. Matthew in the form of a tract. After some delay the New Testament was published in octavo, and of this edition two thousand copies were speedily sold. In 1831 Mr. Bailey obtained two better presses and good type from England; and haviug, with the assistance of Malpan, a Syrian Priest, translated the Old Testament, the Bible was soon issued in three or four volumes. Since that year the publications from this press have been most numerous; and to show their usefulness a list is added of the number of copies printed of each during the past twenty-two years, it being premised that the translations were made by the local English Missionaries. The Bible complete in one volume will probably be published this year (1860).

List of Publications at the Cottayam Mission Press, 1838—1859.

	Copies.
Genesis to Exodus	6000
Gencsis to Esther	5000
Esther	2000
Psalms	8000
Proverbs	5000
Job to Malachi	3000
Old Testament	5000
Matthew, Luke, and John	2000
Mark	7000
Gospels	5000
Gospels and The Acts	8000
Romans	5000
New Testament	12,000
Scripture References	500

	COPIES.
Exposition of the Commandments	400
Exposition of the Sermon on the Mount	100
Evidences of Christianity	500
Collects	500
Hymns	3700
Church Catechism	8000
Watt's First Catechism	23,000
Watt's Second Catechism	10,000
Articles of Religion	500
Important Duties	1000
Sermons	3800
Syllabus of Church History	300
Abridged Prayers	3200
Common Prayer Book	5000
Christian Records	1000
Family Prayers	9000
Peet's Grammar	950
Watt's Scripture History	1000
Amaresum	3000
Bailey's Malayalim and English Dictionary	1000
Protest against Caste	1000
English and Malayalim Vocabulary	1300
Laseron's Dictionary	1000
Outlines of English Grammar	600
Pilgrim's Progress	500
Malayalim Spelling Book	3000
Physical Geography	800
Peet's Geography	500
Atlas	7600
History of India	500
English Fables	500
Tracts	166,200
Monthly Periodicals	73,250
Books for Children	19,050

The measurement of time by the Malabars is arranged in accordance with the astronomical observations of the

Bramhans. The year consists of twelve months, which correspond in the following manner with the European calculations:

1860	Madum *or* Chittray*	April 11—May 11	31 days.
	Eddavum *or* Vaikausy....	May 12—June 13	32 "
	Methunum *or* Auny......	June 13—July 14	31 "
	Carcadaum *or* Audy......	July 14—Aug. 14	32 "
	Chingum *or* Auvany	Aug. 15—Sept. 14	31 "
	Cunny *or* Purattasy......	Sept. 15—Oct. 14	30 "
	Toolam *or* Arpasy	Oct. 15—Nov. 13	30 "
	Vrecheecum *or* Kartigay..	Nov. 14—Dec. 13	30 "
	Dhanoo *or* Margaly......	Dec. 14—Jan. 12	30 "
	Magarom *or* Tye........	Jan. 13—Feb. 10	29 "
	Coombhum *or* Mausy	Feb. 11—Mar. 11	30 "
	Menum *or* Panguny......	Mar. 12—April 10	30 "

* The former name is used in North, the latter in South Malabar.

The length of the months is arbitrarily regulated by the Shastries at Quilon, and advertised by them to the pagodas, whence by the firing of guns and proclamations the arrangements are notified to the public.

The official year is reckoned from the building of Quilon, A.D. 825; so that this is A.U.Q. 1035. In Cochin and Travancore it commences with the first day of the month Chingum, and in British Malabar on the first of Cunny. The astronomical year opens on the first of the month Medum, and New Year's Day always falls within the 11th and 13th April.

The months are divided into weeks, and the names of the days correspond exactly in origin and rotation with our own.

1. Nayar	*Sun.*	Nyaraicha	*Sunday.*
2. Theengul ..	*Moon.*	Theengulaicha .	*Monday.*
3. Chowah....	*Mars.*	Chowahaicha ..	*Tuesday.*
4. Bhoodunn..	*Mercury.*	Bhoodunnaicha.	*Wednesday.*
5. Weeahshum.	*Jupiter.*	Weeahsaicha ..	*Thursday.*
6. Welley	*Venus.*	Welleyaicha ..	*Friday.*
7. Shenee	*Saturn.*	Sheneeaicha ..	*Saturday.*

The division of the year into twelve months, the months into weeks, and the weeks into days dedicated to the sun, moon, and planets, is one of those interesting facts which, independent of other considerations, must suggest an idea of the common parentage of man; and the existence of astronomical tablets showing the correct observation of the Bramhans centuries and centuries ago, together with the recent discoveries of similar tokens of an advanced condition of the human mind in ancient Central America, permit the thought, that at the time of the confusion at Babel man had progressed very rapidly, not only in mighty hunting and in building great cities, but also very possibly in the study of those wonderful laws by which the lights in the firmament of heaven divide the day from the night, and are for signs and for seasons, for days and years.

The further divisions of time are exhibited in this table:

Nody					
8	*Malhran*				
32	4	*Gunnidum*			
320	40	10	*Vinahligay*		
1,920	240	60	6	*Narleegah*	
115,200	14,400	3,600	360	60	Day of 24 E. hours.

So that, instead of making the day of twenty-four hours, each of sixty minutes, the Malabar day consists of sixty hours (so to speak), each of twenty-four minutes.

Some years ago a gold currency existed in Malabar, but the dearth of that metal, as well as the greater necessity for a smaller medium of exchange, have together assisted to render it unnecessary, and the coins are now very rarely met with. Perhaps in no part of the world have such small gold coins been current. The coinage of silver takes place at very irregular intervals, as, since the diffusion of British coined money, the natives have evinced a marked indifference for the debased metal tendered to them by their princes. The Cochin currency consists of cash (copper) of which 10 equal one puttan (silver), and 19¼ puttans equal one rupee. The puttans are very impure, and not only so, but 32 are required to complete the *weight* of the rupee, so that the loss by the above exchange is most serious. In Travancore, on the other hand, the silver currency is superior in purity to our own, but a serious loss in weight is also sustained by the exchange. The coins are cash, chuckrums, and rupees. The chuckrums are employed more or less in the Cochin territory. The Sirkar have declared 28½ chuckrums to be the legal tender for a Queen's rupee; but as the Queen's rupee contains 165 grains of silver, and the chuckrums 557 grains, the just equivalent should be 29·6 chuckrums, or a difference of four per cent., which is of course eventually paid by the country. Chuckrums are the most tiny of silver coins, and very troublesome to count; so the natives use a board, upon the face of which one to two thousand circular holes are cut of just sufficient circumference to receive a chuckrum, and by laying a small heap upon the board, and spreading or shaking the coins about, the little holes are immediately occupied. The fanams are counted in the same simple manner.

The Sirkar accounts are kept in rupees, fanams, and cash, the fanam being, so far as Travancore is concerned, a nominal coin. It is probable that the Madras method of rupees, annas, and pice, will soon be adopted in preference.

The most interesting fact in connexion with the Weights and Measures in use in Cochin is the employment, at the present time, of the old Dutch scales, to the perfect exclusion of the Portuguese tables, and very generally of the English also. In the Custom-house (as in every Anglo-Indian port) the Calcutta weights—

80 tolahs, }
80 *rupees weight* } 1 seer.
40 〃 1 Indian maund (or 82¼ E. lbs.)

are always used for all articles but wines, spirits, and paint oils, which are calculated by English measures. In the Bazaar the scales for most articles, with the undermentioned exceptions, are—

30 Dutch lbs.* 1 maund.
20 〃 1 candy (656 E. lbs.)

FOR SUGAR AND IRON.

25 Dutch lbs. 1 maund.
20 〃 1 candy (546·3 E. lbs.)

FOR OIL,

(which is usually measured in copper pots holding 75 Dutch lbs.)

24 Dutch lbs. 1 chodana.
25 〃 1 candy.

FOR WOOD.

24 borrels }
28½ *sq. E. in.* } 1 tooda.
24 〃 1 candy.

* The Dutch lb.=1·0927 lb. English, or 42½ rupees weight.

The trade of British Cochin has so very recently become worthy of public attention, that the statistics in a subsequent chapter may be rather surprising to many to whom the locality of the port is a mystery. Before, however, entering into those details, it may be well to acquire some practical information upon that tree to which the town is indebted for so extensive and prosperous a commerce; and the cocoa-nut tree is so wonderful a repository of substances useful to man, that a description of a district in which it pre-eminently flourishes would be very incomplete without some notices of its history.

CHAPTER IX.

THE COCOA-NUT TREE.

Causes of Malabar being peculiarly favourable to its production—Modes of planting—The apple—Process of germination—Leugth of life—Employment of the roots for fuel and medicine—The wood—Use of the leaves—Tapping—Drawing toddy; its manufacture into arrack, sugar, cement, and vinegar—The husk—Coir fibre, yarn, and rope—The shell—Kernel, water, and milk—Cocoa-nut oil, its utility to man in all lands.

THE superior character of the alluvian sandy soil throughout Malabar, Cochin, and Travancore has been eminently favourable to the growth of the COCOA-NUT TREE, and the bountiful system of irrigation has promoted its rapid extension. The district besides being benefited by the neighbourhood of mountains is also much advantaged by proximity to the ocean, and a consequent enjoyment of pure sea breezes; whilst the vicinity of the equator ensures at most times that powerful solar heat without which this tree cannot be reared. No tradition is found in India, as in Ceylon, of its introduction. It has doubtless always existed on some part of this coast, and as man travelled south he became acquainted with the shelter and subsistence it so abundantly provides, and was thereby induced to make settlements in the lowlands, and exert his whole strength for its protection and cultivation. Though the discovery of many of its uses has been reserved for modern times, the aborigines of the country must intuitively have understood its local advantages, and by endeavouring to widen their influence have been the active agents in transforming the arid plains of the tropics into lands flowing literally with milk and honey.

The wonderful arrangement of nature by which seeds germinate from the same point, without regard to the position in which they fall into the ground, is beautifully illustrated in the Cocoa-nut. The germ is enclosed in a globular shell of intensely hard wood, and from this shell but one exit is possible, so tiny that it might be predicted but one nut in a thousand would prosper. By the presence of two unfinished holes contiguous to the actual door, one might imagine kind nature had originally intended to afford the sprouting germ three chances to burst through the walls of its prison house. But the tender little shoot has never yet failed to hit the weak point in the shell, and proceeding through a thin horny integument finds itself in a dense mass of fibres, but these being placed parallel to one another, it softly, yet resolutely, forces its way between them, and finally issues into the world. If the nut has been cast by the sea on the sandy shore, or if it has fallen from a tree and been embedded as it lay in the ground, there is a likelihood that the flattened germ end may be lowest in position; but the shoot no less surely continues progressing a little way into the ground, and then starts upwards at an acute angle, making its appearance above ground as healthy, but not so rapidly, as it would have done had it been spared the circuitous route.

The husk has three sides; one is considerably broader than the other, so that if thrown on a smooth surface the nut will always right itself upon this side as a base, in preference to the others. Design is visible in these inequalities, and most planters follow nature's direction in depositing the nut in the ground; for the germ has by this plan to proceed through a greater thickness of fibre, and thus derives a firmer foundation than if it had burst through the apex, as it does when the nut is planted vertically. The latter method has this advantage, that the germ can be watered immediately it issues from the husk, and planters north of Calicut generally prefer it; but those around Cochin consider the horizontal one safer.

It is difficult to conceive that a tree should have its origin from the water and vegetable coating inside the cocoa-nut shell, but this is the case. The water gradually thickens as the internal heat increases, and at length coagulates into a soft ball just sufficiently large to fill up the cavity. This ball, or applè, is occasionally to be seen as a curiosity in greengrocers' shops in London; but here of course it is common enough, and from its delicate flavour is generally much esteemed by the natives, though not by Europeans, who invariably characterise it as similar in taste to elder-pith. With sugar and other seasoning a manufacture of it is made by the native cooks just satisfactory to a man after dinner.

The ripest nuts are naturally preferred for reproduction, and the planter generally selects those from middle-aged trees. He clears a piece of land near his house, and immediately before the monsoon plants them in the soil; perhaps as many as twenty together in a small plot of as many feet square. At the end of the monsoon a little pale green shoot appears from each nut, and rapidly develops by daily watering into leaves and stalk. When six months old transplanting becomes necessary, and the young trees are placed at a distance of twenty feet apart on the sea coast, and thirty to thirty-five feet apart in the interior, where the breezes are not so saline or frequent. The shell is still found quite perfect, and remains so for many years before it breaks and dissipates in the earth around the roots. There are now about a dozen leaves on the tree, each of one piece, but at the end of fourteen months they divide into a number of sections or leaflets, about one hundred and ten on each side of the stalk. This gradual separation is most interesting; no jagged ends testify to hasty workmanship; but, as if cut with the sharpest razor, the pieces stretch from each other with the most mathematical correctness. At eighteen months old the leaflets are about two inches broad and three feet long, and as this is about the dimension of the Palmyra leaflets employed as ollahs, or books, by the natives, the tree is now called "*canakollah.*" At two years old the leaf is of sufficient size to construct a basket capable of containing about twenty-two pounds of grain, and the tree is therefore styled "*cotah-hollah,*" or a "*basket.*" At three years old it is known as the "*annah-chowdoo,*" or "*elephant's foot,*" in consequence of the resemblance of the large bulbous trunk to that huge extremity. At four years old the wood is first apparent above the ground, and the tree named "*marom-*

cundah," or ' *wood seen.*" At five years old* a little horny case, or spathe, sprouts out between the sixth and seventh boughs, bursts on the upper side, and permits the beautiful blossom to issue, on account of which the tree is now named "*chotah-cundah,*" or "*blossom seen.*" And the following year it is called "*tangkah-ittoo,*" or "*cocoa-nut bearing.*" The tree is now matured, and rapidly grows to the height, on an average, of eighty feet. In its prime at about forty-five years old; it then gradually declines until its seventieth year, when the natives cut it down for the sake of the trunk; but if left alone it often attains a century, and at last falls in rotten decay.

In low grounds likely to be flooded by the monsoon freshes, cocoa-nut plants are raised on mounds above the level of the highest rise; and in the subsequent dry weather permanent banks are made by raising earth from one side, and plastering it up tightly against the mound. By this arrangement each bank is divided from that opposite by a narrow canal, which is useful for carrying away the produce. The expense attending the formation of such a plantation is much greater than in grounds where banks are not necessary; but, on the other hand, the trees require no watering, as the canals afford sufficient moisture; and the soil being a mixture of mud and sand retains the moisture longer during the hot weather than the sand alone can do. Ashes and cow manure put to the trees once in a couple of years fully

* In the interior the patient eyes of the planter are frequently not gladdened by the appearance of the spathe before seven or eight years; and if the tope is unfavourably situated with respect to water and breeze, he has sometimes to wait ten years before he has the satisfaction of witnessing the fall of a ripe nut from a tree of his own rearing.

repay the planter's trouble and outlay by the return of heavy crops; and he cannot take too much care to rid the place of weeds, grasses, and small plants, which all require, and derive strength, out of the ground.

It would be vain to attempt a calculation of *all* the blessings man has derived from the cocoa-nut tree, but an account of some of the most striking should suffice to gain it a foremost place among the wonders of nature. It might be well to proceed upwards from the roots as the parts would attract a traveller's observation.

The roots are wonderfully numerous and migratory. In a good soil they are content to radiate from the trunk in a space not wider than the circumference of the many boughs above; but in a poor dry ground they travel onwards in search of more nourishment, and maze themselves with those of neighbouring trees in a most singular manner. With such a hold on the ground, the tree though supporting its greatest weight at the apex remains firmly founded during the fiercest gales; and the winds are seldom successful in uprooting it though they often by simultaneous attack split the trunk in two. On the coast where the sea is encroaching trees are frequently seen with roots almost entirely exposed, and the salt thus imbibed as the waves wash them is most beneficial to the fruit; but on some evil day the water carries away the little bank of sand in the rear, and down the tree comes with dreadful violence, crushing any buildings or smaller trees it may fall upon. It is now an interesting subject for observation only, as to raise so great a length with the weight at the topmost end would indeed be a difficult task in this country.

In clearing away old trees for the sake of substituting

young ones, much annoyance used to be experienced in extracting roots, and the further one mined the more hopeless the operation appeared. But a simple and most effective plan has lately been resorted to, at once to destroy the roots and benefit the soil. The trees are cut off about three or four inches from the ground, and the stumps allowed to dry thoroughly for several days, and then set on fire. The trunks gradually smoulder away, and the roots slowly follow, whilst with their decay the ground sinks in and merges with their charcoal; so when the process is concluded the planter lays a little fresh earth, salt, and manure, and at once inserts the shoots under most favorable circumstances.

The native ironmongers collect the roots washed off by the waves of the sea, and after a careful dryage employ them as fuel where an intensely hot flame is desired in their work. In many parts the tender green roots are esteemed as a satisfactory substitute for areca nut, and a decoction of them with ginger, &c., is considered very beneficial in cases of fever and diarrhœa. The ashes of the burnt roots and husks yield a large quantity of potash, which is much used for the cure of ulcers, besides having considerable employment as soap.

The trunk is striped at regular intervals with rings caused by the fall of the old leaves, and as one leaf embraces its circumference and twelve fall in the year, the age of the tree may be roughly estimated by dividing the number of rings by twelve. Naturalists—sitting before the morocco covered desks in the magnificent Reading Room of the British Museum—in describing the cocoa-nut tree, assert that its age is equal to *half* the number of rings on the trunk; but this is a statement entirely without foundation, and rashly made under the impression that the same rules apply to the growth of palms as of timber trees here, and elsewhere. When sixty or seventy years old the wood is very hard and close, admirably adapted for piles of jetties and bridges; but the molluscs and bivalves, so abundant in the rivers of this country, soon extend their researches into the interior, and necessitate the substitution of such piles once every five years. It is much used as rafters and posts in houses and sheds, cut into slabs for fencing paddy fields or plantations, scooped out for water pipes, &c.; and the inhabitants of the Maldives build tight little vessels entirely with planks of this wood, rigging a mast which originally produced cocoa-nuts at the truck. The middle of the length of the tree gives the best wood; and this carefully seasoned and polished has a very pretty appearance with alternate black and white streaks. It is well known in England as the *porcupine* wood, from its resemblance to boxes made in China and Bombay with porcupine quills.

Tightening the bough's embrace of the trunk is a large piece of closely woven fibre, astonishingly strong and elastic. When the bough has become old enough to bear its own weight, the cloth detaches itself and falls to the ground, whence it is picked up by the natives and used by them for straining various infusions, for snaring birds in the jungle, and, when rolled up tightly, for torches.

It has been well supposed that the arch was suggested to man by his observation of the symmetrical arrangement of the boughs of palms, for there is generally much resemblance in the aisles of a cathedral: the clustered columns, the now subdued, now gushing light, the groined roof, to the view down the parallel rows of cocoanut trees. Perhaps few things are more charming in congregation than these trees, with the morning sun gilding the topmost boughs, brightening the verdant gloss of the middle, and imparting a golden sherry hue to those beneath, whilst the leaflets are defined against the clear pale blue sky like bayonets in an armoury, or hang glistening like stalactites in an arched cave. The birds sing, or rather warble, incessantly; now one passes overhead with a wild note of delight; now another crosses to the opposite tree to join the chorus of his mates; the crows with restless activity making the forest ring with their hoarse notes. At noonday the plantation is insupportably hot, the sun's rays penetrate perpendicularly, and very little effective shade is offered a weary soul; but as evening approaches the shadows lengthen, the breeze whispers comfort down the avenues, the light fails, a gauzy mistiness creeps over the scene, and the trees at length stand out in bold dark relief against the star resplendent heaven. Insects now take up the song that their feathered enemies have dropped; firstly intermittent, as if fearful of discovering their hiding place, they soon acquire confidence; some humming like bees, others chirping like crickets, they unite in maintaining an incessant whirr and buzz throughout a calm night. The moon rises majestically, silvering the motionless leaves and casting those behind into a mysterious grey shade in the most exquisite manner. In the heated atmosphere of the Palm House at Kew a very good idea may be gained of tropical vegetation. The bright polished leaflets, the dense green foliage, the cloudy blue or white trunks, and the long bare symmetrically ringed stalks of a jungle are excellently suggested; and if each tree were allowed more space to stretch its boughs a correct impression might also be derived of the magnificent outline and graceful beauty of the palm tribe.

The trunk is crowned by a bunch of about thirty-five leaves, each on an average twenty feet long and four broad. Looking up from beneath, the arrangement of the branches appears as regular as that of the ribs of an umbrella, and as the leaflets do not grow within two feet of the stem (to allow a space for the fruit to hang) the bunches of nuts and almost all the boughs can be counted. A most singular deficiency is observable in the shadow cast upon the ground by the boughs; the leaflets are most correctly portrayed, but nothing is to be seen of the *main* stalk. This arises from the under part being rounded, and the leaflets being attached in such a manner as to cast a reflection upon each side; these rays falling to the earth cross each other, and the shadow is destroyed.

Twelve leaves would fall naturally from the tree per annum, and the planter seldom cuts away a greater number. On dropping to the ground they are divided down the midrib into two equal sections; these, after three or four days' exposure in the sun, are immersed for about forty-eight hours in water to soften, and then plaited by women into mats of the simplest description. Placed one above another upon rude rafters, and roughly tied together with cocoa-nut fibre, these mats or *cadjans* are almost universally used in this country for thatching houses, sheds, &c., being nearly impervious to rain and solar rays, and yet untenacious of the heat generated in the erection. They are also manufactured into baskets of all descriptions. The green leaf is excellent food for cows and elephants. The natives on festival days are fond of ornamenting their houses, mosques, or pagodas, with chains of the young white leaflets, and attach them to trees on either side of the roads in a most picturesque manner. The midrib of the branch is employed as a paddle, and even that of the leaflet is much used for bristles, toothpicks, pens, arrows, torches and brooms. The natives of Travancore were at one time subject to a frightful torture with it. Around the thumb longitudinally a number of long pieces were placed carefully, bound round tightly with cord, or slips of the leaflet, and when swelling ensued, each piece was drawn out very slowly, causing excruciating agony to the wretched victim.

The spathe is about two feet long at maturity when fit for tapping. On cutting it open a number of small white beans are discovered, beautifully arranged in a lump exactly like Egyptian corn; but, upon carefully abstracting the whole from the sheath, they are found collected in clusters round slender branches which now fall over with their burthen in the most graceful manner. After the case has burst naturally the yellow flowers are thus developed, looking very singular among the surrounding dark green boughs. The pollen of these flowers fall upon and impregnate a few small excrescences at the foot of the stalk, and thus the embryo nut is generated. On an average five nuts are produced from each spathe, and as twelve branches ripen in the year, sixty nuts is the usual crop of an ordinary tree. In the best soil as many as four and even five hundred nuts are sometimes plucked from one tree in the year; but, as the majority may not produce more than twelve to eighteen, the above calculation is always taken as the yearly supply from each tree in the plantation.

The sweet juice, or sap, of the cocoa-nut tree is of inestimable value to the native. The first extraction is usually made when the tree is about eight years old, and the issue, with daily attention, continues regularly twenty to twenty-five years, though generally young trees are only tapped, as the constant bleeding tends to weaken them after some time. The spathe is bound tightly with the pliant leaflets, and bruised along its whole length three times a day for a fortnight, with a bone mallet. The mallet is nothing more than the thigh bone of a bison, the marrow cleaned out, and its place supplied with *ghee*, which, oozing through, greases the spathe when struck and prevents its bursting.

The toddy-drawer, after tapping, proceeds to cut off the apex of the spathe, places a little clay on the wound to prevent the juice trickling through too large a channel, covers it with a small earthen pot, returns twice in the day to cut off another slice and tap, and the following morning empties the contents of the chatty into one that he wears at his side. As he reduces the length of the spathe, the juice, or *toddy*, issues with less readiness, so he generally leaves half of it; and though so much bruising and bleeding has been undergone, the nuts sometimes burst out and ripen on the stunted stalk. About one quart of a milky liquor is obtained from each tree per diem, without reference to the presence of fruit on any other branches; this the drawer waters into nearly four pints, retailing it in the diluted condition to small farmers of the beverage, who also increase the quantity of fluid; and at length the consumers gulp it down with supreme satisfaction. It is sweet, cool, and refreshing before the sun has risen, and, as a mild purgative, beneficial to Europeans. It is almost generally employed in India for yeast in making bread. The poorest natives often take nothing, day after day, but half a shell full at noon, and a quart of *cunghee* (a very thin rice gruel) in the evening. The nut is now so valuable that the low class of inhabitants cannot afford to buy it for food; and as rice is often beyond their means, they would famish in thousands were it not for the bountiful supply of this extraordinary liquid. As the robbery of nuts from the tree is very easy, stern laws have always existed to punish the theft severely; and by fastening thorns around the trunk at night, and making the inhabitants of the plantation responsible for the fruit, the crops are preserved most successfully, though poor famished creatures are listlessly wandering in the shade of their natural staff of life.

After standing a few hours the toddy begins to ferment, and by distillation yields a powerful spirit called *Arrack.* Five quarts of toddy will generally yield one of proof spirit; and as that beverage is always plentiful, and the distillation is effected in half a day, with the assistance only of a few earthenware pots, arrack is at all times abundant and cheap. It is as transparent and colourless as gin, possesses a seducing flavour, with apparently little danger, which, combined with its cost, has made it in large request among our European troops in the North; but the stimulus has induced so much cholera, dysentery, and insanity, that Government is now considering its prohibition to this portion at least of our Indian army. The natives have an insatiable thirst for it, and though its effects are not generally so disastrous to them, yet after excessive indulgence their powers are often entirely ruined by the excitement, and life becomes only tolerable by deeper subjection to the passion.

A coarse sugar, called *Jagghery*, is manufactured from fresh toddy (collected in pots previously limewashed to prevent fermentation) by boiling it down gradually over a slow fire until a syrup is deposited; which poured into cocoa-nut shells, soon hardens into a brown lumpy substance very sweet but rough to the palate. Some praiseworthy endeavours were made a few years ago to refine it for table use, but though the scheme was relinquished, it is to be hoped some means may yet be discovered to provide South India hereby with a commodity of which it is in great need. Mixed with slaked sea shells jagghery forms a beautiful cement, resisting damp, solar heat, and easily taking a high and lasting polish. Columns, cornices, altars, steps, &c., coated with it are made to resemble pure white marble inimitably. Fortifications built with laterite and this cement resist the action of gunpowder most firmly, and when compelled to yield are blown up in huge solid masses, behind which the besieged can still maintain their ground. For facing wharves and quays this plaster is most valuable, and for its durability, facility of moulding, and effect, few compositions are superior.

Toddy is further manufactured into *vinegar* by exposing it in vessels for a week in the sun. The acid thus produced is nearly as pungent as any manufactured from infusions of malt, and is somewhat preferable on account of its freedom from all injurious colouring adulterations. The natives, with the exception of high caste

Hindoos, consume large quantities of it in their curries, and the Jews being compelled to boil sufficient food on Friday afternoon to last them until Saturday evening, employ it very largely in their cookery, and export some six hundred gallons yearly for the use of their Bombay brethren.

The ripe cocoa-nut consists of a green husk about two inches thick covering the hard shell which encloses the delicate fruit and water. The natives tear off the husk with singular dexterity, by striking it on a crowbar or pointed piece of wood placed upright in the ground, and pressing it down obliquely with a jerk. The half husks are at once thrown into a tank of water, or into small pits enclosed with bamboos on the sea shore, and after three or four months' immersion taken out and dried. They are now thoroughly softened throughout, and easily beaten up with sharp strokes of a mallet into pale yellow fibres about nine inches long. The *Coir* fibre, after being well dried, is either employed in the country, or shipped to Europe and America, where it is most extensively used as stuffing for mattresses, for which, from its elasticity and freedom from insects, it is most admirably suited. The fibre is however of most value when twisted into yarn and rope. The manufacture of yarn, which goes on all over the country, as weaving did in England years ago, is simple enough. In a slightly damp condition the fibres are gathered longitudinally between the hands, and twisted into two cords, which are plaited together, more fibre added, and so on. An active woman will in a day make as much as fifty yards of yarn of an average size. In twisting the tight qualities, more time and labour is required; and the hands are so much injured by the hard friction that the fine quality is, and must always be (until the application of machinery) scarce and expensive.

Coir yarn is used throughout India in binding planks, lacing buckets, and for every purpose for which we employ twine. Made up into the well-known coir matting it is now almost always to be seen on the floors of churches, lobbies, &c., in England. Coir rope is manufactured with the rough yarn, in the same manner as elsewhere. Hardly a vessel sails on the ocean without either cables or standing rigging of this excellent material, for nothing has yet been found preferable in resisting the decaying effect of sea water. Its elasticity, lightness, and trifling cost are other great considerations.

The young nuts are never plucked except for food. The water is then a delicious beverage, and the tender kernel, with a little sugar, an agreeable and wholesome diet, in great request during the hot months, and consumed in large quantities on board most homeward-bound vessels. The natives besides introducing the nuts into their curries eat them uncooked, or made into puddings with rice. These puddings are boiled most carefully in a piece of bamboo about one foot long, and when done to the sable damsel's taste are displayed in tempting array between rows of shells filled with the same delicacy. Since the cocoa-nut has been in request for its oil, the natives have ceased to regard it as their chief article of food, for its value quite prevents their indulgence in even one nut per day. They all appear to be very fond of it, which doubtless was not the case when it could be had for asking.

The *milk* of the cocoa-nut is not the liquid enclosed in

the interior, but the juicy moisture contained in the flesh of the undried nut. It is obtained by grating the kernel, moistening it slightly, and then squeezing the mass tightly in a cloth, when a white milk exudes, very agreeable to drink if diluted with a little water. The natives employ this almost universally in manufacturing their own and their master's curry, besides making with the addition of powdered rice some delicate cakes called *oppahs*, which almost always appear on the breakfast table. The milk boiled down slowly changes into a rich oil, also largely used in cookery.

The shell of the ripe nut is broken with one blow of a heavy iron knife into two equal portions, which are exposed in the sun for three or four days to dry up the kernel, and render its extraction easy. For firewood, cups, plates, ladles, and little utensils, the native is satisfied with these half shells. The dried kernels are placed in a mill, and their weight nearly expressed of a yellowish transparent oil. The mill is simple enough; in a mortar, constructed out of the trunk of a tree, a pestle is drawn round and round by two oxen, and crushes any kernels it may meet. The man attending to it feeds the mill slowly until the pit is filled with oil and cake; the oxen are then halted, and a cloth frequently soaked into the oil, and squeezed into a pot by his side until the whole is extracted. The cake is of some value for fattening cows, pigs, poultry, &c., or as manure. The oil is either sold at once to collectors in the country, or brought by the manufacturer himself to Cochin and entrusted to the dealer, who either realizes it on commission, or on his own account. An enterprising firm in Cochin lately applied steam in its extraction, adopting the expedient of turning the mortar round a stationary pestle and draining off the oil into little tubs below.

COCOA-NUT OIL is burnt, from the Himalayas to Cape Comorin, in every palace, church, mosque, and hovel, at christenings, marriages and burials, either in brazen lamps, glittering chandeliers, porcelain vases, earthen pots, or cocoa-nut shells. Since Price's Candle Co. introduced it into their manufactory, it has found its way (as the chief constituent of the composite candle) into every dwelling in England; and more or less penetrated into France, Germany, the United States, and Australia. The astonishing demand that has sprung up in the last few years necessarily enhanced its cost, whilst the production lagged behind consumption; and in India an important addition has in consequence been made to the housekeeping expenses. Indeed plans are being matured for the introduction of gas into Calcutta, as the importation of coal from England, Australia, or New Zealand, and the cost of manufacture would (provided it were generally consumed) afford the inhabitants a much cheaper light than that of oil. But if gas be oppressive in sitting rooms at home, it will be insupportably so in India, where a cool and untainted atmosphere is so urgently required; and though oil may with advantage be expelled from the streets there seems little chance of its losing importance in private life.

The natives employ this common oil in their own dishes, and, unless looked after, act upon an idea that it is the best seasoning for the sahib's food. They anoint their hair with it, and when able to afford the expense, their bodies also. This taste is extremely disagreeable to a new comer, and especially so in Ceylon, where the flavour of food is precisely the same as the scent of the attendant and the odour of the flaring lamp. For protecting the skin from dust, keeping the pores well open, promoting coolness, and for a remedy against many external diseases, it is most valuable. It is often taken internally as a medicine, and a general impression prevails that it might be administered in cases of consumption with most of the advantages attributed to cod liver oil.

There are many things in vegetation which without much study peculiarly strike the observer with feelings of intense admiration and reverence for the Creator's bountiful design, and in proportion as we discover their uses to ourselves we are induced to regard them as superlatively wonderful. Nothing can more induce such thoughts than the COCOA-NUT PALM, whether considered in respect to its agency in fertilizing the sandy coasts of the tropics, to its astonishing growth and perfect symmetry, or to its abundant yield of

> "—— clothing, meat, trencher, drink, and can,
> Boat, cable, sail, mast, needle, all in one."

CHAPTER X.

THE TRADE OF COCHIN.

Influence of the cocoa-nut tree upon the prosperity of Cochin—Evils attributable to the late Mutiny—Reasons suggesting the improvement of the port—Chief staples of the district—The fisheries—Manufacture of fish oil—Ginger; mode of planting, rapid growth, digging, scraping, preparing for market—Horns, hides, coffee, pepper, rice, &c.—Hopes for the future of British and Native Cochin.

To the prosperity of British and Native Cochin the Cocoa-nut Tree has been as instrumental as sheep rearing was to the civilisation of Southern Australia, and though it is quite possible that other and more valuable commodities may be raised in the district, and engage general attention to the prejudice somewhat of Cocoa-nut oil and yarn, it must always be remembered that to those comparatively unimportant articles this part of India is chiefly indebted for what is technically called the "opening up" of the country. Without, however, deferring to the impression general in England that India has only to be *opened up* by railways, canals and roads, to transform it into the El Dorado of the poets, it may yet be believed that civilisation will follow rapidly upon, if not accompany, the extension of inland communication; and it may be reasonably hoped that the increased production of staple commodities will eventually prove a profitable field for the exertions of enterprising Europeans, as well as conducive to the rapid improvement of the legal lords of the soil.

The disastrous results of the mutiny of 1857 are perhaps in no respect so painfully evident as in the necessity now to economise in Public Works, and at first sight it seems unjust that South India, which remained faithful, should suffer for the rebellion of our Bengal army; but it is very probable in future years much good will be traced to the temporary hindrance to these works, especially perhaps in its making sagacious Residents and Collectors more urgent in suggesting reforms to the native princes, and thence obtaining hard earned facilities for promoting those improvements of which the cost might not be so much cared for if the assistance had been given liberally from Madras. There are large uninhabited tracts of most fertile land not one hundred miles from Cochin, possessing every advantage for the production of coffee, linseed, &c., excepting the means of communication with the district around; but as these are being boldly planned, and in some cases commenced, it may be expected that the trade of Cochin will increase in importance every year.

A series of Tables exhibiting the trade of British Cochin for the past twenty years has been appended to this chapter; and also some accounts showing the comparative rates of the chief staple, cocoa-nut oil, in Cochin and London for six years; together with particulars of shipping and ship building in the port. The cost of timber has been so excessive, and the rates of freight so unremunerative that ship-building has lately been almost suspended, but some re-animation is now visible in that trade.

The harbour of Cochin is unfortunately closed during the south-west monsoon. Its conveniences are so admirable that much attention has been given to the (still open) question of the best means of rendering them of value all the year round, and it is generally conceived that with the removal of the mud and sand bar at the mouth of the port that object will be attained. Whilst some advocate a steam tug and rake, others suggest apparently less simple and practicable expedients; but all well wishers to the place agree as to the fruitlessness of merely surveying the difficulty, and Government is *taking into consideration* the various plans laid before them.

The Madras Railway, destined by Government to terminate at Beypore on this coast, should undoubtedly have been differently planned. But the enormous expenses defrayed in the originally designed route must hinder the execution of any new scheme until by experience the error assumes more dangerous aspects. Were the port of Cochin improved as suggested the mails and passengers might be landed or shipped without inconvenience all the year round; and in its present condition the steamers might anchor *at all times* in the singularly sheltered port of Alleppey, whence the water communication to Cochin and thence to Beypore might, at no very great expense, be made amply convenient for flat-bottomed steamers similar to those constructed for the navigation of the Indus.

Of the staple articles of Cochin the oil and fibre of the cocoa-nut tree are by far the most important; their manufacture and ordinary uses have accordingly been considered in the last chapter. The next article on the list is Fish Oil.

The Cochin fisheries are unlimited in extent, and unrestricted. The fishermen reside on the Wypeen side of the river, and at early morning or evening, as the object of the voyage may be, the boats with crews of six or seven men sail out to such a distance as that they may return before night or morning. For some fish, such as shark, porpoise, &c., hooks baited with mullet are generally employed; but for sardines (which are sought in the day-time), herrings, and other small fish, the natives use a parallelogram net about 150 feet long and 12 feet broad. Each extremity is fastened to a boat, and as soon as a shoal is descried every exertion is made by both boats to stretch the net as a fence before the fishes, which, swimming with great rapidity, charge into the unforeseen danger, and strangle themselves immediately in the small meshes. The catch by this simple process is sometimes so abundant as to serve for freight to four boats. The nets and fish are drawn up and thrown into the bottom of the boat, and the men pull lustily home again in the hope of being first in the market. As soon as they land they release the fish from the net, and pile them in large heaps upon the beach. An auction is at once held, and the highest bidder takes the lot. The buyer is usually a Fish Oil manufacturer; if so, he at once has his purchase removed to some rough little shed close by, and thrown into large copper boilers. Salt or fresh water is poured in abundantly, and a fire made below. The water soon boils, and the fish give out their oil, which rises to the surface in globules and is at once removed with a ladle into other boilers. The relics of the fish after being pressed are cast into the sea.

In Ponany and Chowghaut the fish are not landed, but placed in one end of a large boat, and allowed to putrify, to which end boiling water is poured over them once or twice. The oil soon oozes through the sieve-like partition into the other part of the boat, whence it is ladled into chatties or casks. It may be conceived that sickness is always prevalent in the neighbourhood of such stations.

The sardines are in every respect similar to those caught off the coast of Provence, and there is no reason for their not pickling as well. At any rate they cannot be inferior to the sprats in oil which pass for anchovies in places which (like Cochin) are dependant upon London for the "*relishes*" of life. The oil of these sardines is always in good demand, but from the uncertainty of their appearance the trade is singularly fluctuant, as may be seen by reference to the table of Exports.

Herrings are caught in abundance in the neighbourhood. When brought to shore they are gutted, sliced down the backbone, salted, exposed for six or eight hours in the sun, washed on the following morning, dried for three days, and then packed 1,500 together in square mat bundles. These are either sold on the spot at Rs. 3¾ to Rs. 4¾ each, or shipped on a general account to Colombo, where they frequently realise Rs. 9, but sometimes not over Rs. 2 when other supplies are abundant. From Colombo the fish are carried to Kandy and other inland stations, where salt fish is a most valuable and almost necessary article of food.

Prawns, small lobsters in appearance, are caught like the herring and sardine in parallelogram nets. They are simply dried in the sun, packed in robbins, which contain 25,000, and shipped to Colombo, where they realise generally most profitably for the shipper.

Sharks are very rarely netted, in consideration of the valuable net which a large fish generally succeeds in ruining. They are brought to shore, and cut up without delay. The head is useless. The liver is boiled down, and one to three chodanahs of a thick oil obtained. This oil is used to adulterate the sardine oil, and to season the wood of new boats. The flesh is cut into pieces about one foot square, salted, packed in bundles of three hundred, and shipped to Ceylon, where it is largely consumed by the lower classes. The fins are salted, shipped to China, and there boiled down for the sake of a rich gum they are said to contain.

The Ginger shipped from Cochin is chiefly that produced in the Chernaad district, near Calicut. The plantation is made by natives upon tracts of ground rented from Government, or private individuals, at the rate of Rs. $\frac{3}{4}$ per maund of seed, or for about nine maunds green ginger raised. In May the seeds—small roots cut away from the fresh ginger—are planted at one foot apart in ground cleared and prepared for the purpose. The shoots appear in three or four days, and the monsoon rains stimulate their growth. In October the leaves begin to fade, and in November they wither away entirely, and the planter is thereby warned to dig up the roots. The spice at this stage is dark, bulbous, and unsightly. The natives scrape it carelessly, rub sand and ashes over it, and expose it in the sun for four days. About 75 per cent. of the prime weight evaporates by this process, and the spice shrinks into the thin, brown, rough-skinned staple known as *Native* Ginger.

The preparation of the article for the European market is much more careful. The spice is scraped and trimmed immediately after extraction from the earth; washed three times in fresh water; spread in the sun for three days; covered from the night dews; scraped again; soaked in lime water, with which a small quantity of sulphuric acid has been mixed; placed in baskets in a brick-bleaching house; and exposed to a sulphur vapour for one or two hours. It has now to be thoroughly dried, carefully sorted according to certain qualities, and packed in cases for shipment. By this process 80 per cent. of the prime weight evaporates; but the extra loss and the expense in the preparation is generally amply remunerated.

Horns and hides are collected in all parts, but the chief rendezvous is Changanacherry, a most populous inland town about fifteen miles south west of Alleppey. The horns are also collected in large quantities near the jungles, and people are constantly employed seeking for the pieces of which the deer and buffaloes are sometimes deprived by being entangled in the trees. Spotted deer's horns are very valuable, as their solitary much resembles that of ivory.

Hides are staked, and now generally salted before exposure to the sun; but partly on account of the leanness of the animals, as well as owing to the carelessness with which the carcases are dragged about, the skins are seldom of superior quality.

The slaves are allowed to have the bodies of those animals which appear to have died a natural death; so when the demand for hides is active they frequently poison the cattle on the estate for the sake of the skins, which the Jews at Changanacherry are always ready to buy under such circumstances.

Croton seeds are produced in Allway, Cottayam, and many other places in the district. They are retailed from bazaar to bazaar, until finally they accumulate in Cochin. Coffee is raised without difficulty in similar spots, but to no great extent at present, the export being that grown in Mangalore and prepared in Cochin. Pepper is a monopoly of the Sirkar, as is also bees-wax. Both are smuggled into British Cochin in small quantities. Rice is cultivated in the low swampy lands around the Backwater, but this sort is generally consumed in the neighbourhood, the article exported being of Bengal production.

Such is Cochin; the site of the European's first settlement in Hindostan; the witness to the last struggles of the Portuguese and Dutch for supremacy in the East; and the theatre at the present day of those masterly reforms of native regal rule, which must tend by degrees not only to increase the trade of the district, but also to promote a thorough improvement in the character of the natives of South India. Public attention has lately been painfully drawn to the condition of this continent; and apprehensions of danger impending from our present incertitude of action have thereby become general, and it may be difficult to conceive that Cochin and Travancore have brighter days before them; yet everything favours the hope that the deeds that have disgraced these countries, and checked their progress for centuries, are now rendered impossible by the liberal honest rule inaugurated by the recent change of the advisers of each Rajah. The little spot of territory which we own at the entrance of the Backwater is situated most happily for the freedom of coast traffic, and the prosperity of neighbouring kingdoms; let the advantages of the locality for trade, for rapid postal and passenger transit, for the defence of our hard-earned possessions, be rightly valued, and we shall not be disappointed in our hopes for the future of British and Native Cochin.